Family Secrets

Family Secrets

By Jean M. Walker

ISBN-13: 978-0-9988558-0-6

Edited by Margie Kay

Published by Un-X Media
PO Box 1166
Independence, MO 64052
www.unxnews.com

Illustrations by Neriah Barrett
Photos copyright Jean M. Walker

Front cover art:
3D rendering of an alien hushing© Sarah Holmlund-fotolia
Smoke- clipart.com

Cover design by Margie Kay

Published in the United States of America

Acknowledgements

Dedicated to my grandparents, parents, and loved ones who
all have given me so
much guidance in life and from the beyond.

To my brother, Ted. I could not have written this book
without his help and input.

To my many friends, who encouraged me and put up with
me during the writing process.

Thank you to Neriah Barrett for working diligently on the
illustration for this book. Neriah is a very talented high
school student and the granddaughter of my friend Douglas
Barrett.

Thank you to Margie Kay for working so hard on the editing
of this book. I am also grateful to her for encouraging me to
write this book, and for her guidance in the fields of the
paranormal and ufology.

Special thanks to my best friend Claudia Perry for her help
with editing and all her encouragement. Claudia is a special
person who has a heart that is full of kindness and love. I
thank her for a lifetime of friendship and sisterhood.

To my Star Child son, Tommy, for giving my life purpose.

Jean Walker

CONTENTS

Jean Walker

Foreword

Jean Walker's story is unique, intriguing, and worthy of further investigation. In this book, Jean tells her tale of strange paranormal events that occurred during her entire life. I've known Jean for several years and have had the opportunity to work with her on a number of UFO, cryptid, and paranormal investigations. We have become good friends and often spend time together outside of our investigative work.

I've always found Jean to be extremely serious about finding answers to not only her own strange encounters, but other's as well. She keeps digging and doing site investigations to get as much evidence as possible. With a background in science, I can depend on her to always try to find a mundane explanation for a strange event before she categorizes it as unknown or paranormal in nature.

There are many people who have experienced a lifetime of weirdness, but few have the courage to let others know about it, much less use their real name on a book. Jean should be commended for coming forward after 70 years of living what most would call abnormality, to let the others know that they are not alone in their experiences. I suspect that if everyone came forward with their story it would help greatly in getting answers to what is happening but most don't for fear of ridicule.

After completing over 1,000 paranormal and UFO investigations, I can say now that I am certain that there is not only *something* going on, but a *lot* of something going on that science cannot yet explain. In Jean's case alone, we find extraterrestrials, shadow people, spirits, a crop circle, strange creatures and a portal in or over her house.

There have been manu strange events occur along 39th Street in Independence, Missouri. So much so that it is known as the paranormal highway among researchers. Most of the activity involves sightings of unidentified flying objects, orbs, missing time, and paranormal encounters. For some reason, most of the witnesses who have spoken to me have a background in law enforcement or science. Is it a coincidence that Jean's first house where she had early encounters with strange creatures and aliens was on 39th street?

It is likely that since Jean and I have experienced many of the same things we understand each other better. It is nice to be able to sit down and talk about something bizarre with someone else and not have them look at you like you're out of your mind. I also find it odd that many of us who have strange experiences seem to accidentally run into each other. Many people have investigated UFOs, and some, like J. Allen Hynek, started out as skeptics and finally concluded that there is indeed some type of visitation occurring. Many others, such as Bud Hopkins, Stanton Friedman, Linda Moulton Howe, Debbie Ziegelmeyer and her brother, Chuck Zukowski, and Chase Kloetske, to name just a few, who have taken this seriously and devoted their lives to finding the truth. Nearly all ufologists have become aware that even after years of research they keep running into road blocks and advanced technology that is difficult to understand. We only have bits and pieces, and while we know more now than in earlier years, it gets ever more complicated as time goes on.

There is so much evidence available in the form of video, photographs, physical injuries, radiation evidence, electro-magnetic field evidence, and other trace physical evidence, that for me there is no question whatsoever that there are aliens or inter-dimensional beings visiting our world daily. I've personally seen all of this and more, and now realize that we must look at quantum physics and higher dimensions if we are to gain any kind of understanding of the phenomenon. This includes spirits and cryptid creatures as well, who may also be interdimensional beings.

Jean is an example of perhaps one of "their" experiments, or studies. Whoever they are, they are extremely intelligent and very technologically advanced, and it is unlikely that outside of our black ops government agencies the public may never understand what their ultimate mission or goal may be, but it is obvious that some people are being used for genetic experiments and as incubators for hybrid beings.

Some feel that disclosure is imminent. There are signs that this may be true, however, I will remain cautious if and when this happens because I don't entirely trust anyone, especially beings from other worlds, and certainly not our government, who has keep this secret since the 1940's or earlier.

Why is it that it seems some people are singled out for such experiences? Is it just a coincidence that a portal is located right at Jean's house? She had experiences as an infant and child in an entirely different location, but when she moved to her current house 45 years ago, the strangeness continued. Was the portal placed over her house on purpose, to make it easier for whoever or whatever to come and go as they please through dimensions? These are all questions that need answers, and I'm sure that Jean will continue to pursue her investigation into these matters with the help of others, and I look forward to working with Jean in the future.

Margie Kay

Jean Walker

Introduction

I am writing this book for several reasons. One reason is that I have difficulty trying to talk about all the things that have happened in my lifetime, and writing about it is much easier. Writing allows me to put things in a chronological order, which helps me to recall things better. I have found that writing this book has helped me remember all the odd things that have happened.

Another reason for writing this book is that I hope to reach others who have had similar experiences so they know they are not alone, and that they are not crazy. Many people have had similar experiences, but not everyone wants to talk about it. There has always been, and still is such a stigma concerning UFOs, abductions and paranormal occurrences. I hope that in some way my book will give others some comfort. It is also my hope that together we can figure out the truth about what is happening to so many people around the world.

This book is true to the best of my knowledge. There are no exaggerations or fabrications. I simply try to put in writing many of the things that happened to me and my family. It all started back with my great-grandmother and continues today through my brother and myself. We, like many others, have questions about these experiences. Why do some families have a lot of psychic, paranormal, and extraterrestrial contact? Is it hereditary? Is there an interest with certain blood lines or DNA? I try to explore some of these questions in this book.

Chapter 1

It all started with Great Grandma Nettie

I woke up out of a sound sleep hearing voices and smelling smoke that was coming from behind me. It was about 2:00 a.m. and I was sleeping over at my Grandmother Nellie's house. I was sleeping on the couch in the living room with a very large cuckoo clock hanging on the wall in front of me. I was hearing voices. I laid there, frozen for a while, trying to get awake enough to figure out what was going on. There was a large street light right outside the huge open window that lit up the living room very well. I got my nerve up and jerked up. turning around in fright to see who, or what, was there. Then I heard my Great Grandmother Nettie's voice saying, "It's okay honey, it's just me." She was sitting in her platform rocker chair right behind me and was just rocking and talking.

I was only seven years old and this was a very startling way to be awakened in the middle of the night as I was hearing a very strange conversation going on. I just laid there for a while watching the smoke do curls in the light that was shining in through the window.

I was wondering why my great-grandmother was up in the middle of the night smoking, and who she was talking to. There was no one in the living room but the two of us, and I had been fast asleep. I could tell Nettie was not talking to me. Grandma Nellie (Nettie's daughter) was still asleep in the other room so there was no one else to have a conversation with.

A little bit of family history here: Grandma Nellie was Nettie's only child and Nellie had one son, Theodore, who was my father. I finally fell back to sleep while listening to my great grandmother talking as though she was having a conversation with someone in the room other than me. I remember thinking, even at such a young age, how crazy all this seemed.

The next morning I was having breakfast with grandma Nellie and I told her about Nettie waking me up and her talking in the middle of the night. I said, "Grandma, there was nobody there in the room with us. Who was she talking to?" Grandma Nellie just kind of threw her head back and laughed at me. She said, "Well your Grandma Nettie is just very different from most people and she was talking to her spiritual guides. She gets up most nights to smoke and talk with them." I thought, *what the heck are Spirit Guides- and why couldn't I see them?* But I didn't question grandma Nellie any more about spirit guides until I was much older.

I really did not understand what the term "spirits" were at this point of my life. I couldn't wait to get home and tell my Mom and Dad what had happened. I was very concerned for Nettie's mind. This story was no surprise to my parents, and they were not at all shocked at my story about Grandma Nettie. My parents then tried to explain to me what had been going on with Nettie getting up and talking to no one in the middle of the night.

Mom and dad started telling me how Nettie was a "psychic" and how she had special abilities to see things that most people could not see. I think it was my mother who told me "spirit guides" were spirits that helped Nettie see things that other people could not. Mom said guides were just that, they guided you through life and tried to help you with decisions. However, these guides were spirits and only grandmother Nettie could see them and talk to them. It was a bit difficult to understand at that age, but I did get the general drift of what they were trying to explain to me. I remember that I never looked at Grandma Nettie in the same way again. Instead, I saw Nettie as someone who was very special and had special abilities that most people did not. I looked at her in awe and wondered how she acquired this special talent.

While growing up I begin listening closely to the stories my dad told about his grandmother Nettie. My dad's father died when my father was only seven years old. Nettie's husband had passed away with cancer many years before. So both Nettie and Nellie were widows and they lived together raising my dad. Growing up with both his mother and grandmother in the same house, dad knew a lot about the strange things Grandma Nettie could do and about her special talents.

Nettie was born Nettie Gibson, but always went by her married name, Morrow. She became a well-known psychic in the Kansas City, Missouri area. Nettie was recruited by radio stations to talk about her psychic abilities. She would sometimes help people who called in to the radio station with problems they had by using her psychic abilities. There were several newspaper articles written about Nettie and her psychic abilities, and how Nettie helped others with her gifts.

Nettie also had match covers made up for advertisement to give away to people. Many people smoked at that time and it was common to advertise in this manner. I do have one of the match covers but have been unable to find any copies of the newspaper articles, even though I heard about them quite often. I also have a small leather pouch where Nettie kept some Chinese coins that she would use to help contact her spiritual guides. Grandma Nellie told me Nettie would take two of these coins, holding them in one hand and rubbed them together as she went into her trance. I think the coins were just more for concentration than anything else.

Nettie told her daughter, Nellie, that she had two strong spirit guides. One was a Native American Indian princess who passed away when she was around twenty years of age. Nettie seemed very close to this young princess and would talk with her most of time. Her other spiritual guide was an Indian from India. Nettie said he was very old, even ancient, and she said he was not too up to date on our modern world. However, she said he was a large man and had a lot of physical strength to help and protect her. She said he was a very useful tool for her in the spirit world. Grandma Nellie told me their names but I am afraid I've since forgotten them. I found out that these two guides were the ones that she had been speaking to when I woke up in the middle of the night.

Many people would come to Nettie and pay her for the helpful knowledge she could provide. One day a lady called her because she had lost her wedding ring, which she was heartsick about. She asked Nettie if she could tell her where the ring was and Nettie went into a trance. Nettie told her to go out on her front porch which was made up of small boards laid together.
She told her which two boards to look between to find her ring. They hung up and the lady called her back in a few

Nettie at age 18

minutes and sure enough, she found the ring. She told Nettie it was exactly where she said it would be and then she sent Nettie money for finding it.

Great Grandma Nettie was very attractive in her younger days. She once won a beauty contest at the Missouri State Fair when she was eighteen for being the prettiest girl at the fair. She won a large portrait of herself, but it was later destroyed in a fire. Thank goodness, they had copies made which I still have. After Nettie's husband died she was still very pretty but grandma Nellie said Nettie would never date another man. The only man Nettie ever wanted in her life after being widowed was her grandson, my father. Like most grandmothers, she thought the sun rose and set in her grandson.

I got used to Nettie's strange ways. She would often say things out of the blue about stuff that was going to happen, and talked to people the rest of us couldn't see. She passed away when I was nine years old, but I still remember her vividly, probably because she was so different and special.

Grandma Nellie kept Nettie alive for me by sharing so many of her stories. I once asked Nellie if Nettie ever said anything about me or about my life, as I was the first-born Grandchild. She really hesitated, but finally said that when I was very young Nettie said that I was going to suffer a lot of heartache in my life. Well, I still am not sure what she met by that because I think most all of us suffer a lot of heartache. However, I have had my share of sadness for sure, some of which I will talk about later in this book.

Grandma Nellie told me how Nettie would hold séances in her dining room. I need to describe Grandma Nellie's scary house at this point. This is a recent 2016 photo of the side of

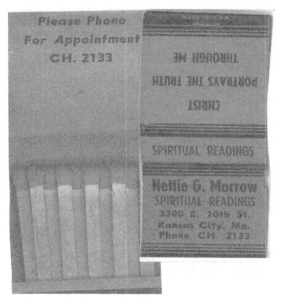

the house. The first window to the right is the living room window where I slept on the couch. The side door is the one that her tenants used to enter to access their apartments. Her house sat on a corner lot in Kansas City, Missouri. It towered on a small hill and it was three stories high, plus a basement. If you entered by the front of the house, you had go up several flights of stairs. It had a large front porch that had pillars. Grandmother lived on the first level.

The interior solid walnut stairway was gigantic. On the first landing was a huge set of windows facing the west that were just beautiful. She had two apartments on the second floor and one on the third floor. The ceilings were very high with beautiful walnut trim top and bottom. Dividing the living room and the bedroom were two solid walnut doors that would slide open from inside the walls.

On the other side of the bedroom, which led into the dining room, were two more walnut sliding doors. The woodwork in this old house was just gorgeous and looked like what you only see in movies now.

She had one bathroom, the kitchen, and a very small bedroom behind the kitchen. Grandmother rented that small bedroom to a man friend of hers, while she and Nettie shared the other bedroom. As a youngster, I found this house very scary with so many floor levels to it. There were nooks and crannies everywhere. The house was so huge, that as a small child, I found it very intimidating.

There was a dead-end stairway that grandma used for storage and she called it Fibber McGee's closet. For those of you too young to know who Fibber McGee was, this was a popular radio show in the 1940's about a man named Fibber McGee and his wife Molly. They had this closet that Fibber would use to throw everything into. It was a nightmare to find anything in. When Fibber would open the closet to find something, you would hear all kinds of banging and clanging as a bunch of the stuff would just come falling out of it.

Grandma Nellie's house Photos: Jean Walker

Grandma's closet was right off the main hallway in her part of the house; the hallway went from the kitchen to the living room. She used it a lot like the closet on the radio show by just throwing things in there that she didn't know what else to do with. There was a little bit of everything in that closet! Remember this closet as it will be important later in this book.

In the huge dining room grandmother had a very large rectangular shaped dining room table made of solid walnut. The chairs were made of heavy walnut like the table and covered with red velvet for the seats. Nellie told me many times during séances Nettie would place her hands on the table and levitate the table about four to six inches off the floor! No strings or wires, no tricks to it, she would just raise that heavy walnut table!

The family sitting at the heavy walnut table

My dad added to this story by telling me that when he was growing up many of his friends would tease him about his Grandmother. They would say she was crazy and that no one could really do the things like predict the future, levitate furniture, or make the spirits rap on the doors and windows. One day my dad was tired of being teased so he asked his friends to join him with his grandmother at the heavy dining room table and to hold a séance. Nettie agreed to do this for him because she knew his friends were teasing him. His friends agreed to do the séance with Nettie thinking it was all just a joke.

One evening several of dad's friends came over and they all sat down with Nettie at the table for a séance. Dad said Nettie went into her trance as he sat there with three of his friends. Then the table started to move slowly and it started to lift off the floor while it rocked backed and forth. He said once she had the table off the floor it began to tip a little and she started asking the spirits to knock on the front door. At that time the knocks started coming from the front door which was not that far from the dining room. Dad said the other boys turned white, jumped up from the table and ran through the kitchen and out the back door! He said not only did they stop teasing him but they didn't want to talk about what had happened that night. He said they didn't call Nettie crazy anymore either! Dad sounded very pleased about the reaction he got out of his friends and about how Nettie had pulled it all off.

My Grandmother Nellie told me that it became apparent when Nettie was a very young child that she had a psychic gift and she was a little different from others. She told me they would sometimes call her "Crazy Nettie." Nettie's Mother would prepare lunches for the men who worked the fields. She used to ask Nettie "What field are the men working in now?" Nettie would stop and concentrate for a minute and then tell her mother where the men were working. Grandma Nellie said Nettie was always right and

Nettie's mother always knew where to take the lunches for the men.

It is terrible that Nettie had to live with people calling her crazy throughout her life just because she had this great psychic gift. We do a lot better in understanding this now but even so there is sometimes a stigma attached to it. I think Nettie's psychic gift was the real
reason why she never remarried. She worked very hard to make ends meet on her own. She owned a restaurant for a while and cooked or waitressed when necessary. She did whatever it took to survive in those hard times during the depression era and beyond. I am proud of her because she was honest and hard working.

Grandmother Nettie

Nettie did what she did with her psychic ability and she didn't worry about what others thought.

I feel Nettie was quite content to live with her daughter

and grandson while she worked on helping others with her gift. She was a Christian and said Christ worked through her to help others. I can still remember when someone would get sick in the family Nettie would call Unity Church asking for prayers and she would pray for others. Yes, Nettie was a very spiritual person. As Nettie aged, she liked her wine and sometimes drank more than she should, and she smoked. However, back then everyone smoked. I remember how neatly dressed she always was, and she was still a pretty woman for her age. She passed away in 1955 from complications from a gallbladder removal operation. Great grandmother Nettie was the first person in my family to pass away in my lifetime. I really didn't understand what death was at that time or quite how to accept it.

My mother, Marie Leffler, and father, Theodore John Myers, got secretly married when they were both seventeen. At nineteen my dad joined the Army Air Force and fought in World War II. He learned to fly in the Army Air Force and was the Sergeant over a crew of men in a B-29 bomber. They were bombing over Germany when my dad's plane was hit

Ted & Marie Myers

and went down, and as he was falling through the air he awakened and pulled his ripcord. Dad said when the plane was hit by ground fire it was burning and then there was an explosion. He was then knocked unconscious and the force blew him out of the plane. Dad said, just before the plane exploded, he was lying on the floor of the plane with his face on fire, he said he felt God holding him at that point. Somehow, he had managed to get a parachute on before he was knocked out. He said he woke up as he was falling.

The Germans shot dad twice as he fell through the air, once in the hip and once in his foot. He injured his back (he thought he broke it) when he pulled the ripcord. His face and hands were burned from the burning plane. He said as he fell through the air, he saw his plane go past him. The pilot was still at the wheel and he went down with the plane. The pilot was a good friend of my dad's, so this was additional stress to bear. The only other person who survived from the plane crew was my Godfather, Frankie Plesea, who was the gunner in the bubble right under the plane.

Dad said when he hit the ground, the German soldiers ran over and kicked his helmet off his head. They asked him what his nationality was, he and he told American German, which was the truth. He said he thought that was the only reason they didn't kill him on the spot.

The Germans were dragging the American soldiers that were shot down through the streets. The German women were boiling big pots of water and throwing it on the captured Americans as they were dragged through the streets. Dad said as bad as this sounds once he saw the destruction

Sgt Ted Myers

of what the bombs had done he couldn't blame the German women for what they were doing. He said small German children were lying dead in the streets along with many adults, their homes were destroyed and there was total chaos everywhere.

He said it was one thing to be in a plane dropping bombs and quite another thing to see first-hand the destruction and death they were doing on the ground. After all, my dad was only nineteen years old at the time and not prepared for what he was experiencing.

Once captured, he thought he was the only one to have survived from the plane crew. The Germans were using a church as a hospital for the wounded Americans. One warm and sunny day they took the men from church hospital who were lying on cots and set them out in grass yard in the sunshine. Dad rolled over and to his surprise there lying next to him, was my Godfather, Frankie. He said Frankie had a large hole in his chest and one in his leg which the Germans had just stuffed gaze in, but he was alive. Later, after Dad had done some healing, they put him in a German prison camp.

The Germans moved dad and other prisoners several times from one prison camp to another in railroad cars. Dad said the cars were full of holes and it was freezing cold outside. Many of the prisoners froze to death or got sick and died. He said one time he really thought he was going to freeze to death but he found a pile of prisoner's shoes in the railroad car. He piled the shoes on his head and body to keep him warm enough to survive, which he did.

My dad was in a German prison camp for nine months and weighed 95 pounds when the Russian's moved in and the German's deserted the camp. Dad said the men in the camp tore the barbed wire fencing down with their bare hands to get out. He said they didn't want to wait for the Russians to get there, they just wanted out!

From Germany, dad was flown to France, where he recuperated from his wounds and ordeal of imprisonment of nine months. This meant that for nine months no one at home knew if he was dead or alive, all the family knew was that he was missing in action. He was finally able to contact his family once he got to France for further recuperation before coming home.

Dad's mother and grandmother were just heartsick with grief from worrying whether Ted was dead or alive. Grandmother Nellie told me this story many times and I will not ever forget it. She said Nettie had enough worrying over Ted and she told Nellie she was going to find out if Ted was dead or alive by using her psychic abilities.

Nettie went into the bedroom and pulled the large walnut sliding doors shut on both sides of the room. She instructed Nellie not to bother her under *any* circumstances. Nettie had pulled in her favorite rocking chair, her cigarettes, and some water into the bedroom. She pulled the large, thick, green, velvet drapes closed across the windows. Nettie was now ready for her psychic journey to begin!

Grandma Nellie told me that Nettie was in that room for three days straight with no food or sleep. She said she would put a tray of food outside the door and Nettie never took any of it. Nellie said she became very worried about Nettie and wanted to check in on her. However, Nellie remembered how sternly Nettie had said, *"Don't bother me at all! No matter what, don't disturb me!"*

Nellie said when Nettie finally came out of the bedroom she looked a wreck! Nettie had to have been about 70 years old when this happened. Nettie hadn't eaten anything and had little or no sleep. Nettie told Nellie, "Ted is alive. If I am wrong about this, then I will stop all my psychic dealings from here on out."

Nettie said, "I see Ted walking on a bare, wide board, and he is carrying a tin plate. There is barbed wire fencing right next to where he is walking on the boards. He is going to get in line for some food."

Nettie said, "Then I see him on a bright and sunny day running up our front stairs from the street. He is taking the steps two at a time and yelling, "Mom, Grandma, Mom, Grandma", and he has some happy news for us!

Nettie was so correct in what she saw in her psychic journey. My dad came home to Kansas City, Missouri in the summer of 1945. My parents had been married for seven years with no children. Then just as Nettie had described, on a bright, sunny day, my dad came running up their stairs, two at a time. He was yelling, "Mom, Grandma, Marie (my Mother) is pregnant!" Then he would repeat this over and over as he climbed the stairs. I was born May 7, 1946 and my brother, Teddy, was born April 3, 1948. Grandma Nettie was proven right again with her psychic abilities, and saw what others could not.

"Christ Portrays the Truth Through Me."

Nettie Morrow, Spiritualist

Jean Walker

Chapter 2

Through the Eyes of the Children

The first twenty-nine months of my life we lived with my mother's parents in Independence, Missouri. Effie and Web Leffler were the best grandparents a child could ever have! As you can tell, I loved them dearly and they loved me equally. I thought I was the luckiest child in the world because I had two mothers, Marie and Effie. I truly did not know the difference and I called them both mama. I didn't figure out one was my grandma until we moved out to our own place when I was two and a half years old. My grandparents lived on Maywood Street in Independence until they passed away, so they lived there for many years. My mother was born in a hospital but my Aunt Margie, mother's sister, was born in that house.

The Maywood house was small (2 bedrooms and 1 bath), but we managed. My aunt Margie was living in the house with us- she was in and out of the house as she had a troubled marriage. One of my first memories happened in that house when I was around one year old. I was in my crib and it was night time when I looked up at the most frightening face I had ever seen! For years, I thought it was a scary clown face staring at me. It had a whitish gray face with large black eyes. It had no hair and it was bent over my crib just staring at me. I felt like it knew it was scaring me and it didn't care. It had a mocking smile that scared the heck out of me. How frightened must a child be to remember something like at such an early age?

When I got older I told my mother what had happened to me in the crib. My mother's answer was, "Oh that was probably Margie with a lot of cold cream on her face." I was crazy about my aunt Margie and I think I would have recognized her and not been scared to death. Now knowing what I know about aliens, I feel it was my first encounter with an extraterrestrial. That would explain why after all these years I still remember the event in great detail. I think they chose me at an early age for abduction, which would continue throughout my life. This is the only time I remember ever being afraid at my grandparent's house. I spent a lot time staying with them through the years and their house was like a refuge from the world for me. I always felt safe and loved with them.

I have read in numerous places that aliens are often mistaken for owls or clowns. That explains a lot as I look back upon my life events.

My dad purchased an acre of land on Crysler Street in Independence. It was about 10 to 15 minutes from my grandparent's house on Maywood. It was very rural in the area when my dad first bought the land. There were several farms around us with lot of woods and ponds. It looked nothing like it does today, nearly 70 years later.

My dad hired the farmer who sold him the land to dig the basement out using a team of horses. My dad built a basement with concrete blocks and the roof was just flat with tar on it. I can still remember when it rained we had to put buckets under the leaks until Dad could tar the roof again. I guess we were poor but we didn't know it! We had one bedroom and one bathroom, which we were thankful for. The four of us slept in the same bedroom, my brother and I in cribs and our parents had a bed. It was a small, but cozy room with a walk-through closet that had two doors. You would think we children would not have been afraid with our parents sleeping so close by, but we were afraid and for good reason. The house was haunted! We lived right on the path of the old Santa Fe Trail where it went through Independence, Missouri. When the neighbor next door dug out his basement, he found an old headstone of a young girl. They felt that because of the date on the stone she must have died on the Santa Fe Trail and her family most likely was traveling in a covered wagon.

When I was about four years old my mom would put my brother Teddy and me to bed and then join my dad in the living room to watch television. I could hear something under my bed and it would mumble. I could sense with everything in me that it was evil, and not a nice creature at all. Then I finally got so I could see it. It looked like nothing I had ever seen before in my short life. It was black with white rings around its eyes and it looked similar to a monkey. It had a long tail and I named it Bosco, although I don't know why. This small creature walked on two legs. The creature was bipedal and about the size of a monkey, maybe two to three feet in height. I would curl up in my crib making sure that no of my body parts dangled outside over the crib mattress. I felt that it could not hurt me as long as I stayed in a ball in my crib. But it was living under my bed!!!

After months of being tortured by this Bosco creature, I got up the nerve to tell my mom about it and about how scared I was. She laughed and said it was just my imagination and that I needed to just stick my hand out of my crib when it was under my bed. She said, "It won't hurt you because it's not really there!" Mom said if I did this, I would get over the fear of it and that way I would know it was just my imagination.

I worked up my nerve one night when this Bosco character was under my bed to stick my hand out of the crib. I slowly slid my little hand out over the mattress and my fingers

BOSCO

were just dangling there. Then all of a sudden something bit my hand. It felt like a dog bite when it would just snap at your hand and not do any great damage, but it really hurt!

I just wanted to scream and I think I did, "I knew he was real, I knew it, I knew it!" To say the least, I was not happy with my mother! I told her what happened, but she paid little attention to what I was saying about it. I think she looked at my hand and said, "Oh, it was probably Lady who bit you." Lady was my cocker spaniel who never slept under my bed and she never bit anyone! She was blond and so sweet, not like that black Bosco creature. I don't remember how long Bosco tormented me, but I think it was a couple of years before he left me alone. Now I wonder maybe if he was an alien and not this freaky creature I imagined, and he stayed under my bed to keep an eye on me, or maybe to prepare me for something else in the future. I don't know what Bosco was, but he frightened the hell out of me!

My mother was adamant about my brother and I taking naps because of the polio scare, which was spreading across the country like wildfire. At that time, it was thought that getting plenty of rest, like taking naps, would help to ward off polio. So in the afternoons, we had to lie down and mom usually lay with us for a nap.

I was a bit of a hyper kid and often could not go to sleep in the afternoons. I remember many times laying in the bed and just looking at the wall. It was then that I saw strange things on the wall. It was as if the wall was a movie screen and I watched two men in prisoner style striped uniforms sitting on their bunks. The scene was always close to the same thing and I could tell they were having conversations with each other. The men would talk to each other and smoke cigarettes. The scary part of this was that sometimes they seemed to be aware of me watching them and would look right at me as if they could see me. However, I did not ever feel they were going to hurt me, so I was not afraid of them. I just wondered who the heck they were and what they were doing.

Sometimes the two men would be sitting together on the

top bunk and sometimes one man would be on the top bunk and the other man on the bottom bunk. If they were not sitting on their beds, they would be just walking around the very small cell talking to each other. I remember their beds were made mostly of springs, big springs with a small mattress on top of them. These scenes would just play over and over like a movie seemingly with no point at all to them. This was just another weird thing that happened to us during our childhood.

My brother Ted, who is two years younger than me, says he remembers seeing these same men. Ted said he could see the cherry red on the end of their cigarettes and they had an old hound dog lying with them. I don't remember the dog but could have forgotten that part as it was a long time ago. Ted also says that he is not sure if their outfits were stripes or confederate uniforms.

I guess it could have been confederate soldiers that were imprisoned, perhaps on our land at some time in the past. In my mind I remember the men wearing striped prisoner's uniforms. Ted said one time he was watching them and one of the men looked at him and then waved at him!

After thinking about some of these strange happenings, I had a vision about the large oak tree we had right at the opening of our basement. I could see in a vision that it had been a hanging tree. As I have learned more about different paranormal happenings, I suspect that this "movie" we kept seeing was most likely a residual type of phenomena that was taking place over and over. This residual type of time imprint sometimes happens in haunted houses where spirits keep doing the same thing over and over. Perhaps at one time, there was a prison on our property and some of them were hanged at this old oak tree right next to our house.

I never wanted to be alone in that basement house. I could feel and see spirits around us all the time. There seemed to be something going on constantly around us and I could feel it. As a child I could not explain what I was seeing or feeling, but now I know it was spirits, and sometimes evil entities. I could sense Native American Indians and visualized them dancing around a fire. I would feel the anger and fear the Indians had toward the white people. I also felt their fear of starving to death and the harsh weather they had to endure in our area. In other words, I could feel their suffering and sometimes I could see them. Guess I am somewhat like Nettie after all.

Ted tells me he also would see men running in a counter clockwise direction with black stripes on their clothing. This sounds to me like he was seeing Native American Indians running around a campfire or it could have been confederate soldiers being made to run in circles. My brother tells me, he could often hear men's voices coming from behind the headboard when he was in bed with mom and dad. Maybe what he was hearing was Indians chanting and that is why he couldn't understand what they were saying. Again, I think this could relate back to the time period of the Santa Fe Trail and the fact that we lived right on it.

The worst of my memories were that I could really sense the evil forces that were living with us. They were always taunting me and my brother because we were so vulnerable to their presence. Poor Ted, he suffered the most with the fear of these demons. He was truly tortured by them more than I was. I think I found ways to shut them out but Ted never could, so he grew up living with these torturous fears almost daily.

My brother told me that devil-like creatures started tormenting him when he was about three years old. Ted would be lying in his bed at night and he would hear an evil laugh like, "Ah, ha, ha, ha." He said it was always late at night around midnight and he would see this evil looking man coming at him. This man looked as if he was Chinese descent with slanted yellow eyes that had a black pupil that ran vertical.

Now tell me that does not sound like a pure demon! He said this "thing" had sharp pointed teeth and it would give out with its scary, evil laugh. The thing would appear over the top of Ted as he lay in bed. Then it would fall on him going all the way through him as he laid there helpless in his bed. Ted was totally terrified!

Ted said he could only see half of its body (the upper part), and its hands had claws, which it would hold up in the air while diving at Ted in bed. Ted told me it was at this time he would start screaming bloody murder and mom would get him and put him in their bed.

Dad added a bedroom and washroom on to the basement house. Mom and dad moved into the new bedroom which was right next to our old bedroom. My brother and I were still sleeping in the old bedroom. There was no hallway between the bedrooms you just walked from one room into the other bedroom. Our bedroom had the walk-through closet with doors at each end of the closet. Ted tells me that one night he saw this demonic looking entity come out of the closet of our bedroom. Ted was standing next to his bed when this entity came out of the closet and it looked right at him! Then it floated into the back bedroom where our parents were asleep. He said it had on a robe, and had no feet. It was just very wispy on the bottom and transparent. He said the demon hovered over Mom and Dad and then it just dropped down right over our dad's body!

The above picture is the basement before dad added on the back rooms. The large oak tree is to the left that I suspect could have been used as a hanging tree:

"So many horrid ghosts!"

William Shakespeare

Chapter 3

The Big Move and Devils

When I was nine years old my dad had completed building the upstairs part of our home, so we moved from the basement to the upper level where my brother and I had our own bedrooms, which was very nice. My bedroom faced the north side of the house, and right under my two windows was a small roof, which was over the main door to the basement. The large oak tree or the hanging tree was right outside my window. Sometimes I would just crawl out on the small roof and look at the sky and enjoy the warm nights. Dad then rented the basement out for extra income. The basement had eight rooms with a bath and its own entrance and driveway, so he got a fair amount of rent for it.

I remember that Teddy was still tormented by "devils" as he called them, and he lived in constant fear, even after moving to the upper level of the house. Teddy would sleep with heavy covers over his head, even in the hot summers, and we did not have air conditioning. Mom would go into his room in the mornings and pull the covers off his head and he would be covered in sweat.

I felt so sorry for Teddy, but there just wasn't much I could do about his fears. I remember one time, Dad was talking about Teddy being so scared of the devils and he said, "Maybe Teddy is just such a good person and that's why the devil torments him." Teddy was a good little boy while I was the ornery one and always getting into trouble. To this day, Ted has a very sweet nature about him and is full of kindness.

Now, after doing UFO research, I wonder if Teddy wasn't being abducted and he thought the "Greys" were devils! Sometimes peoples' minds (and we were just children) just can't handle being abducted by aliens, so they associate the aliens with something they do know about. In Ted's case, he knew what devils were so that is what he saw- devils, not aliens. I really have a strong suspicion that knowing what I know now, this could have been what was happening to Teddy.

There were a lot of advantages for children growing up in a half-suburban and half-country atmosphere. There was always something to do outside and Teddy and I lived outdoors playing. We had a lot of undeveloped acreage around us and a pond right at the end of our acre of land. Our backyard sloped downward to the pond. My dad built a barn and fenced off about half an acre so he could buy us a horse. For many years, Mom would plant a good size garden, which we would all help work in. We enjoyed eating our fresh food from the garden. Almost all of our neighbors had large gardens and did a lot of canning and freezing. Summertime was a fun time for us kids and we enjoyed growing up in this atmosphere.

Following page: This was the Crysler house while being built, front view and back view. Note the open breezeway that we would sit in at night and view the sky.

Notice how the back yard sloped down to a pond (not shown).

The neighbors living to our north built a barn and bought a calf every year and he would butcher it when the cow matured. He would butcher the cow by hanging it from the tree right outside their house which was between our houses. This really grossed me out and I tried not to be around that area much when it was butchering time. The neighbors who lived to our south raised chickens. One of the pet chickens named Betsy loved to ride on our horse Penny's back. It was so adorable to watch a horse and chicken befriend each other. The same neighbor with the chickens also kept beehives and collected honey.

The reason I am explaining all of this is to let the reader understand the environment in which we lived.

"The horrific nightmares I kept having seemed too real. Who are these monsters that are coming after me?"

Brent Oldham. Children of the Greys.

Chapter 4

Fairies and ETs

As a child growing up in our neighborhood, we had lots of places to roam and explore, which we did often. We had lots of fun at the pond watching tadpoles turning into frogs, frog hunting, riding horses, playing with animals of all kinds and exploring the fields. We were only 10 minutes from the Independence square, yet our lifestyle had all the quality of living in the country. Today all the ponds and fields are gone, filled with houses and other developments.

Dad had built the upstairs part of the house with an open breezeway and the garage attached to it on the other side. We lived on a hill and could see parts of downtown Kansas City lights and towers. We would spend a lot of time sitting in the breezeway during the summer evenings watching the skies, and it was cooler there in the summers. We would watch the big cumulus clouds build up and the storms as they came in from the west. We had a great view from our house with no trees or obstructions to block the scenery.

Often, we would be watching the sky at night when strange lights would appear. A couple of times, (maybe more) we saw saucer-shaped objects flying. UFOs were often seen by us, and by that I mean lights and shapes that we could never identify. My dad was a pilot and had his own plane. He loved to sit outside with us and sky watch. Even dad would say things like I wish I knew what that thing is up there in the sky. I remember several times dad getting very excited at we were seeing and say, "What the hell is that? That's no plane or blimp!" Dad was not easily fooled and I now know that what we were seeing were UFOs. I can remember him getting a bit upset about some of the flying objects we were seeing.

Several times I saw unexplained lights in the fields behind our house. They were unusual looking small white lights, usually one light at time, and they would move slowly around the fields then just disappear. I still wonder about those lights and what they could have been as they appeared to be more like floating lights moving through the fields. It always reminded me of the story of the Headless Horseman who was looking for his head because of the way the lights would move around as if they were looking for something. That part was just my imagination and part of being a child but the lights were real. I was too scared to go down into the fields by myself at night to chase them and see what they were. Most likely I would not have ever been able to catch them anyway because they did this disappearing act so quickly.

This was the time period in the 1950's when there was a lot of speculation going on about aliens and UFOs. Roswell had become a hot topic at the time and many, many, people were seeing UFOs. This included my family, as we saw a lot of suspicious lights and crafts from our place.

I remember one warm summer day I was playing in an empty field next to our house. The field was full of wildflowers blooming and there were butterflies everywhere. There were groups of beautiful butterflies of all colors and they were gorgeous! I have never seen that many butterflies before or since that time. I remember even then I thought how unusual it was to see so many butterflies at one time. The number of them had to be in the hundreds and there were all different species of them flying together.

I sat down on the ground watching these beautiful butterflies flutter around the flowers and grass. I still, after all these years, remember how delighted I was to witness all these beautiful flying creatures. I have always loved and felt close to nature (I guess that is why I became a Science teacher). Then, among the many flowers, I started seeing "little people." They were "fairies"! There were just a few of them at first but then several others started showing up. It was like they knew I was just enjoying the beauty of nature and would not harm them. They actually let me see them!

They were running around, and seemed so jolly and happy just wanting to play. They were dressed in little bright colored clothes and there were about a dozen of them in total. The fairies would run around the flowers hiding under the petals of flowers and chasing each other between the tall grasses. They wanted to play with me! I remember thinking how beautiful all this was and how I enjoyed playing with them. I had been running around among the butterflies, but when I saw the fairies I just sat down on the ground and played with them, all the time still watching the beautiful butterflies. I even remember thinking how this was really a unique experience and that other people probably wouldn't believe me if I told them about this event.

I think I was about seven or eight years old when this happened. I do not remember seeing the fairies again, but what a great time I had! I knew they had trusted me enough to come out into the open where I could see them. I remember they were so happy and so much fun to play with because of their jolly personalities; they just made you feel wonderful.

The only other time I recall seeing little people was before the neighbors built the house to the south of us and it was just an empty, overgrown field. I used to run through a path on this property to the nearest neighbor's house to play with the children. One hot summer day, I was on my way home, crossing the overgrown lot and there was a stump in the middle of the lot. As I was walking on the path I looked over at the stump and there were about three little elves! They were playing or doing something on the top of the stump. They looked right at me and they had a very surprised look on their faces as if they were surprised I could see them. They just stopped and stared at me as I was looking at them.

I was as shocked to see them as they were to see me, so while I was looking at them, I just slowly kept walking toward my house. They looked a lot like the little gnomes we see in the stories and buy for yard ornaments, but I would call them very small elves.

I have read that pixies, fairies, and elves all fall into the same category along with the "little people". The belief in the little ones goes way back in history to Ireland, Britain, and Europe. The Irish have very strong beliefs in leprechauns and the wee people, even to this day. I also have a lot of Irish blood in me so maybe that is why I could see them. I have recently heard that fairies who appear to people could be connected to ET's. This belief goes along with and could help explain the many other things that have happened to me in my lifetime. So maybe it wasn't such a crazy thing for me to have seen these little people.

I recall a conversation with my mother and grandmother (her mother) as a child. They were talking about fairies and pixies and they sounded as if they believed they were real. It could have been that a child's book I had at the time about fairies had that started that conversation as I remember it. I wish I could recall the conversation more, but I was young and don't remember all of it. I did get the general idea that they had seen them around grandma's house. I remember another time when it was just me and my mother, she told me she had played with fairies as a child and I really don't know if she was kidding with me or she really did see them. So if fairies are part of the ET's world, that would explain a lot as to why I was seeing them, along with my Irish heritage.

I talked to my friend, Margie Kay about this. She is a renowned psychic and remote viewer. We spoke about fairies one day and she told me that some people think fairies are ET's and that the tales of old tell of kidnapping of children and babies by the "little people," which may refer to abductions by extraterrestrials. Wow, that just so hit home with me and I wonder if they have something to do with my being abducted since I was a child.

I have been working a case in Eastern Independence that has had a little bit of everything happening in it. I plan to write a book on this case, but still have more investigation to do on it, which hopefully, I can complete in a couple of years. I have one picture I took at this place and it looks just like a fairy. You can see the outline of her wings, her head, arms and legs as she flies around.

I have included one of the pictures – see what you think about it.

Possible fairy is in the upper left hand corner.

"And as the seasons come and go, here's something you might like to know. There are fairies everywhere: under bushes, in the air, playing games just like you play, singing through their busy day. So listen, touch, and look around-in the air and on the ground. And if you watch all nature's things, you might just see a fairy's wing".

Author Unknown

Chapter 5

Childhood Terrors

While we had a lot of fun growing up in this country environment, we had many scares too. My brother's terror with demons and devils continued throughout his childhood.

I felt so sorry for him and the trials he was put through with these "devils." I had my own terrors and fears which happened not only at night, but during the daytime too. Teddy and I played a lot down at the pond behind our house. There were wild foxes living in a den next to the pond with cattle and horses in the field. However, when I would be playing there, I always had a sense that *something else* was there and it was always watching me.

What a terrible feeling for a child to grow up with...it was always there. I was always looking over my shoulder and sometimes I would see things darting quickly out of my sight. This only increased the fuel to my insecurities of being watched all the time. It wasn't only when I was outside playing, but in the house too. I knew *they* or *it* was watching me. Although in the house, even though I felt someone was watching me, they were outside and not in the house with me. However, now I know that at night they did come in the house for me.

As I kept looking over my shoulders through the years, I

begin to see a humanoid form that would quickly dart behind anything near it to hide from me. I did not understand what this entity was, but I did understand that it was nothing good, nothing that I wanted to have following me around. Now I was able to make out that it was a humanoid form and it was for sure chasing me, but I knew it was not human. This thing would follow me, hiding behind bushes, trees, houses, etc., but the worst thing was, even if I wasn't outside it was still watching my house!

Sometimes I could see this entity from the breezeway in broad daylight. It would be in the back of yard by the barn. I saw it quickly jump into the barn one day; it knew I had seen it watching my house, looking for me. This humanoid had on a shiny, silver suit or coveralls that even its head was covered. I could not see a face just all covered with this silver shiny suit. Now I know it looked like an astronaut type suit, but I could not make out a face. One day, I was walking up the hill from the pond to the house, which was a good incline to climb. Suddenly, I felt this creature following me and I began to run up that hill with all my might. When I got to the house I finally had the nerve to look back and I saw it dart into the barn again. My heart was pounding when I reached the safety of the back door.

That evening, I told my parents over supper what had happened to me that day with the spaceman chasing me. My dad said he would take a look in the barn to see if everything was okay, and it turned out to be fine. Then my parents kept telling me it was just my imagination working overtime. They tried to calm me saying I was safe now and no one was going to get me. I kept telling my parents someone was going to take me- over and over I would tell them this. Now as a mother, I think that would have scared me to death if my child had told me such a thing. However, they didn't believe me; they thought it was just my imagination.

I kept having the feeling over and over, that someone was not only watching me but they were going to kidnap me. I just felt like, okay, I know this thing is going to get me. My dad was a gun collector and we always had loaded guns in the house.

My dad used to take us kids hunting often and I did know how to shoot a gun. Even having a gun in the house didn't help me feel safe. It was as if I knew that a gun would be useless in this situation and this humanoid thing was going to take me away. Where? I don't know. I didn't feel as if it was going to kill me but it was going to take me away from my family. Maybe it would hurt me. I didn't know. In today's world, things are so different and children are in harm's way often. However, when and where I grew up it was different, and we didn't even lock our doors. Yet I lived with this great fear of being taken from home.

I saw this entity that I referred to as the "spaceman"

Humanoid creature in the ban and shiny sparkles in the pond

(because of the shiny silver suit) so many times when I was outside playing. He was always there, always some place close and always watching me. My brother and I were recently talking and he said, "Sis, I remember when we were kids and playing hide and seek with the other kids in the neighborhood. You would often run up to me and say, "Did you see him? The spaceman - did you see him? He is chasing and following me all around. Did you see him?" Ted told me, he could tell I was scared and very serious, but he himself never saw the spaceman. But then, he did see devils!

One day, Teddy and I were outside playing down close to the pond. It was a sunny, warm day during the summer. I saw the spaceman by the dam part of the pond when I was in the pasture. Then the spaceman disappeared over the dam towards the water. This time I mustered my courage up and ran towards the area where I had seen him. When I reached the pond, to my surprise, he was not there any longer but in the water there were circles. The circle was in rings like when you throw a rock straight down into the water. I stood over the edge of the pond looking down into the center of the circles and I saw, silver shiny sparkles in the in the center of the ring. Silver sparkles like the suit of the spaceman and it was sinking slowly, slowly, to the bottom of the pond.

This scared the hebe-jeebies out of me and I left the pond quickly and headed for the house. The spacemen had the capability to go under water and stay there! I have never forgotten that day and most likely never will. I just couldn't grasp or get a hold on what was happening to me with this "spaceman". What was he? What did he want with me? Was he really going take me away? Was he going to hurt me? So many fears to grow up with, and so many things I could not figure out.

Now I wonder if there couldn't have been some kind of craft in the water that the spaceman was staying in and that's how he stayed hidden most of the time. This would have been a perfect place to hide when he needed to and would have allowed him the ability to watch me. The pond was right behind my house and he could take me when he wanted me. Perhaps he was from one of the motherships and he would take me to the mothership in a smaller craft that was hidden in the pond. I now feel in my heart that was really what was happening.

But, what did an alien want with a child? I was only about nine or ten years old when I started to notice the spaceman. I remember him being there for at least two years. By the age of eleven, I was terrified to sleep at night. I was constantly telling my parents that I knew someone was going to take me! I had two windows in my bedroom and I remember my parents being upset about my intense fear of being taken. I recall my dad saying to mom, "Maybe we should put iron bars on Jeannie's windows. Perhaps that would calm her down and make her feel more secure so she will be able to sleep at night." This never happened, but now I know that iron bars would not have stopped the spaceman or my fears.

I think the spaceman and his kind had some definite plans for me and my life. They were using me to produce hybrid children and I have the feeling it wasn't just one type of alien taking me, but perhaps several kinds. I will cover more about the different types of aliens and why I feel I was taken by more than one race of aliens later in this book.

"Nothing is more frightening than a fear you cannot name."

Cornelia Funke, Inkheart

Chapter 6

Unexplainable Things and Night Flights

So many things happened to my brother and me as we were growing up, and they still continue to this day. One very unexplainable thing I recall is when I was about 10 or 11 years old, I had a bright purple scar that ran from the top of my pelvis bone about 5 inches up on my stomach stopping an inch or so below the belly button. It looked as if I had had a major surgery. But it was only at this age I remember it showing up. I had a girlfriend spend the night with me and she saw me undressing and asked me, "What is that scar on your stomach?" I just looked at her and said, "I don't know where it came from." I had wondered about this scar previously, but my friend seeing it and asking me about it really started me thinking about it. I wondered where it came from and why no one ever explained it to me. I knew I never had a surgery that I could remember and I thought surely my mom would have told me if I had had a major surgery as an infant.

Now this is a really strange incident. I asked my mother while showing her my scar, "Mom, how did I get this scar? Did I ever have a surgery?" She just looked at me and said, "No, you never had a surgery. Don't worry about the scar, it's nothing. And no, you never had a surgery." It was like she really couldn't see the scar at all or she sure wasn't going to acknowledge it at all! Then she said, "You don't have a scar so just stop talking about it." Wow, I am standing there with my pants pulled down showing her my scar and she was saying, don't worry there's nothing there, just stop worrying about it! Now that is just weird!

My only explanation as I think about this now, is that the scar was there because my friend saw it but something (perhaps aliens) was keeping my mother from seeing it. I think they didn't want her to become worried about it and maybe take me to the doctor, so they wouldn't let her see it. They had plans for my female organs a little later in my life.

I experienced many strange things I did not understand as child. At the same time in my life that I was so afraid of being taken by something, I also discovered I could fly at night. When I would get into a sound sleep I would leave my body and fly outdoors. I could feel myself lift out of my physical body and then look down upon myself sleeping.

This is known as astral projection, astral travel or out-of-body experience (OBE). There are many names for it, but it is believed to be a soul-flight where a person leaves their physical body behind. I would then fly through the window (without opening it) and discover the beautiful sights of the night. I never flew very high, just over the treetops or buildings. I loved sailing through the air and the great freedom I felt with the flying. I just loved to do this.

I would discover many animals roaming around and would follow them. Birds, owls, foxes, raccoons, rabbits, squirrels, even cats and dogs, if they were out there. I have always loved animals of any kind and felt a real kinship to them.

On my night flights, I felt like I had a special connection with the animals whenever I came in contact with them. It was like I loved them so much and they loved me back, and it was a special love. When I was out flying around my favorite thing to do was to play with the animals. The animals would know I was there just right above them and they did not run or show any fear of me. Sometimes they would just run around in a very playful way with me. The best time for night flying was when there was a full moon. The moonlight was so beautiful, it lit everything up in such a soft way and I could really see the animals well. From what I can remember, I almost always saw owls on each flight. Now I think I know why I was always seeing owls, because owls are associated with Extraterrestrials.

I also enjoyed seeing the city lights at night, but it was at a distance as I never went too far from home except when following cars sometimes. The lights in the houses below me always gave the homes a warm, appealing look about them. It was so fun watching automobiles traveling with their headlights on, especially if they were traveling down a dark road, as most of them were where I lived. Most of all I just loved the freedom of being able to fly anywhere I wanted to go. I would soar up and down, fast and slow, it was such a fun and free feeling.

When this first started I didn't realize that I could control as to when and where I would fly. Then I started thinking about it and if I hadn't flown for a while I would just tell myself I was going to fly that night. Sure enough, the night I would decide where I wanted to go flying that is what happened to me. I would end up flying and right to the place that I decided to go!

Sometimes I ended up in strange places, though. Places I didn't recognize, although they were always beautiful. But, remember I didn't like to fly off too far from home. Some of the places reminded me of a fairy land or like nothing I had seen here on Earth. Maybe the term "magical places" would describe it better. These places were not scary, just unfamiliar to me. So perhaps all of my astral flights were not here on Earth.

I only did this for a couple of years, and then I developed this fear of not being able to get back into my body. It scared me and I was afraid I would die if I continued with this flying, so I stopped it. Just like that, I stopped doing it. Many years later, I would try to do it again but the fear of leaving my physical body behind is way too scary and I can't seem to do it.

These out-of-body experiences were very pleasant for me at the time. I felt light, free, and in contact with everything around me. In most countries and religions, you can find a belief in astral projection. The Bible speaks of the silver cord in the final chapter of Ecclesiastes (14) that could well fit in with this belief: "Before the *silver cord* be loosed, or the golden bowl be broken, or the pitcher be shattered at the fountain, or the wheel be broken at the cistern." I do not know how I learned to do this OBE but it happened so naturally for me.

On the other hand, perhaps it was taught to me by some other source, such as ET's. I even had the thought that perhaps the ET's used my love of animals to get me outside to do this flying so I wouldn't be scared. Perhaps I wasn't flying solo but had the ET's with me and that's how I was able to fly and it felt so natural to me. Or maybe I was just doing astral projection and leaving my physical body all on my own. I may never figure the truth out on this, but it is one of the reasons I would like to be regressed.

Ted's Near Death Experience

My brother told me that he thinks he had a near death experience (NDE) when he was nine years old. He was sick and running a high fever, so needless to say, he stayed home from school that day. Both mom and dad had to go to work and I went to school, leaving him home alone with a high fever. I still do not know or remember why mom didn't have me stay home with him. When this happened to him, he thought he had had a bad dream and people back in that time knew nothing of what NDE was or how it happened. Today, my brother is sure he had a NDE.

He found himself looking in the mouth of a cave. This cave had a glowing, amber light coming out of it. There was a dirt road between him and the cave and he seemed to be just floating across the road. He tells me, he was not walking but he was "floating" through this event the entire time. When he entered the cave there were three or four old wooden steps on both sides of him. He went down the steps into a large room with stone on the floor. It was now dark on both sides of him and he floated to an edge, where he saw a very large giant who was standing on a balcony!

This giant was at least 18 feet tall with a huge, white face. Its large eyes were closed and he had long, whitish/gray hair with no neck to him. It looked like he was so round his head just sat on his shoulders, with little or no neck and the giant had a huge chest. The giant wore a black robe and Teddy was hovering right in front of him. Teddy turned at a 90-degree angle and saw four human figures wearing dark colored robes. The robes had hoods on them and the hoods were covering their faces. Teddy turned around and faced the huge giant who was about ten feet in front of him and the giant still had his eyes closed. Teddy said at that point he woke up and he was covered in sweat, which he thinks was caused by his fever breaking.

This was a wild story, but Ted swears he was so sick, he knows he died and had an after-death experience. Ted says he knows now that Jesus was carrying him and that is why he felt as if he was floating!

About 22 years later, Ted happened onto an article in a magazine while waiting for his wife at a doctor's office. This story was about a patient who had died and had an after-life experiences. This patient saw a very large man on a balcony and there was a line of people waiting to see him. The giant would grab a person - lifting them up to his face and looking them directly in the eyes. Then the giant would throw them down into the darkness off to the side of the balcony. We assume the giant was throwing them directly into Hell. The darkness was Hell.

The giant could see in their eyes what kind of a person and soul they possessed. The giant was the Gate Keeper to Hell, his name was Apollyon (which is found in the bible) and he was the head demon! In the bible, Jesus made the giant give him five of the keys to Hell. This man in the article said Jesus was showing him there is a Hell and there is an afterlife.

Ted said he was just breathless when he read this article, because of all the similarity to what had happened to him as a child. He said that this article was just so close to what he had experienced, he knew it had to be the same thing happened to him. Ted felt it was like God was saying, "Yes, this really did happen to you." Ted is sure that his experience was for the same reason as the man's reasons were in the article- that Christ was showing him there is a hereafter and there is a Hell. I know in my own heart there is a hereafter, and the Holy Trinity and Hell do exist.

I believe my brother is correct in his belief of this happening to him. Jesus led him to the truth and perhaps these devils that were in his life knew he was saved, so they just kept tormenting him.

In yet another strange experience for my brother he heard

something others could not. My mother's parents were from the small town of Vienna, Missouri. Her relatives were farmers and lived in the country outside of town on farms. Mom had several cousins living in Vienna and they often visited each other as children.

Mom took Teddy when he was about fourteen years old on a trip to Vienna to visit relatives. During the visit, they decided to go out to the local cemetery to pay their respects. Ted said when they got to the cemetery, they got out of the car and started walking up to the graves. Ted said he started hearing a piercing scream of a woman that sounded like she was in great distress! He said nobody else in the group appeared to be paying any attention to the screaming. Everyone just went on walking and having a normal conversation with each other.

Finally, Ted spoke up and said, "Don't you guys hear those terrible screams of that woman?" He said everyone just looked at him in dismay, but no one said anything and they just continued to walk on at a normal pace. Teddy was shocked at everyone's reaction, or lack of reaction, to the screaming. Ted finally grabbed mom by the arm and said, "Mom, don't you hear that woman screaming?"

He said mom turned around and grabbed his arm and walked a short distance from the other relatives. Mom told him, "Shut up. What is wrong with you? There is no woman screaming. If you don't shut up everyone is going to think you are crazy. Go back and sit in the car and wait for us there." Ted said he went back to car but he could still hear this woman's terrible screams that didn't end until they drove out and away from the cemetery.

My mom, bless her soul, sometimes would just ignore what she didn't understand. Ted said she never mentioned the incident again to him and he never brought it up to her. How was it that only Teddy could hear these screams? I guess he was the only one sensitive enough to hear her agony. This would be a frightening event for anyone, let alone a teenage boy. It leaves me wondering, who was this woman (ghost) and why was she screaming like that?

"How can you know what you are capable of if you don't embrace the unknown?"

Esmeralda Santiago, Conquistadora

Chapter 7

The Baby Stealers

I am sure the house on Crysler street in Independence was haunted, and not just the house, but the property the house was built on. Everything about that place was strange and I can't help but wonder if that area was not a portal. A portal to the past, present, and future to include aliens and space ships. This would explain so many of the happenings there.

I got married way too young at the age of sixteen, but that was not all that uncommon back then. I quit school without a high school diploma. I wanted to feel safe and start my own family, and that was all that was important to me at that time of my life. I think now that one reason I wanted to get married was to get away from my house. My husband was only eighteen, but I did feel save and loved with him. He was a hard worker for a young man and he would strive hard to support us. He too, had no formal education and so he used his strong back to work.

We were a young couple struggling to make it during hard times. We were married in 1962 and it was a wild time in the world. Hippies, drugs, rock & roll, President Kennedy and Robert Kennedy assassinations, Watergate, UFO cover ups, all kinds of government cover ups, and the worst thing of all was the war in Vietnam. It was a tough, unsettling time. We struggled a lot with things, but truthfully, we were so busy trying to make it in the world we didn't have time or the inclination to party or do drugs.

So, I think it may have been a good thing I got married so young and wanting to start a family. I wanted to be a good wife and mother, keep a clean house, and be a superior cook! In today's world that doesn't sound like much or maybe it's just that women can't afford to stay home and really have the time to do those things. Today's women have careers, which is a good thing, too. It was just so different than the time when I grew up. Later in life, I became a career woman and after furthering my education.

With practically no money to even feed ourselves, my husband and I decided to rent the basement apartment from my parents. My dad gave us a cut rate on it but my husband and I did a lot of work on the place. My husband got into construction work building bridges and it was very dangerous work, but he liked it. His whole family was in the bridge building business.

After several years passed I finally became pregnant for the first time. I was just deliriously happy over it. The one thing I wanted more than anything on Earth was a child! The doctor ran the tests and I was pregnant, things were looking very good. I was so excited and couldn't wait until the baby would be born. I always felt the main reason God put me on this Earth was to be a mother. I felt this way with every morsel in my body. I was meant to be a mother!

At about two months into the pregnancy I started having problems. I would have sharps pains in my stomach and I started spotting. I knew this wasn't a good thing. Then at three months I started having labor pains and the bleeding got much worse. The doctor told me to stay off my feet, stay in bed and get up only to use the restroom, and I followed his orders. The pains got much worse, and I passed some stuff that I thought was the baby. I had to take it into my doctor to be examined.

Heartbroken, I went to see my doctor with the jar of stuff I had passed. The doctor said "I know you thought this was the baby, but it was only the afterbirth." So I asked the doctor, "What happened to the baby?" The doctor said, "Well I'm not sure but sometimes nature just takes care of that kind of stuff." How strange indeed! It was my first pregnancy so I really didn't understand everything that was happening.

The doctor felt it would be best to do a D&C in the hospital because it would clean my uterus out and help me to get pregnant again. So I had it done. Anything that would help me to pregnant again. After the D&C the doctor told there really wasn't much left in me and there was no fetus. At that time, I had to believe what the doctor was telling me about no fetus remaining, but even then I had some serious doubts.

Now I wanted a baby more than ever, I was so worried that I would never be able to have a child and would be left childless all my life. I was a very small boned young lady and only weighed around 110 pounds. I had constant female problems- pain, bleeding, and many more problems than I should have had for my age. About a year later, I got pregnant again. I had the rabbit test and all that they could do back then, and I was finally pregnant again!

But things were not going to go well. At three months gestation, I miscarried again. I spotted throughout the pregnancy and had a lot of pain. I tried to stay in bed as much as I could and prayed and cried a lot because I could tell how the pregnancy was going. This time I just bled heavily, I didn't pass any afterbirth or fetus. Again, they did a D&C and again they didn't find much left in my uterus as far as tissue or a fetus.

The third pregnancy went in a similar fashion. It took a much longer time to get pregnant, but I finally did. This pregnancy went just like the last one, miscarried at three months, had the D&C they found little to nothing in the uterus. This story is getting old and was heart- breaking for me to go through because each time I would get my hopes up, only to have my hopes destroyed again.

The fourth pregnancy was somewhat different. By that time it was getting more difficult for me to get pregnant. I had my tubes blown out, took birth control pills for three months, then would stop taking them to see if I would get pregnant. We tried the birth control pills several times but nothing happened, it just didn't seem to help me get pregnant. I even tried some of the newer fertility pills that could cause multiple births, but nothing happened. No pregnancy. I did the temperature chart where you take your temperature before you get out of bed and when it went up a little you were ovulating. That didn't work either, so then the doctor put me on some kind of hormone shots for a while and then stopped them.

I had just about given up hope when I got pregnant again! This time it felt different than the other pregnancies. I didn't spot near as much and I carried the baby into the fourth month. I really thought I was going to make it this time and have my baby. I went into the doctor for my regular monthly examine and was feeling okay. My stomach was even pouching out and I was starting to look pregnant. The doctor did an examination on me and I can remember what he said like it was yesterday. The doctor said, "Jean, something is wrong and the baby is not growing anymore. I am sure it is gone." I felt as if I had been shocked and my heart just crumbled into pieces, because I just really, really, thought I would make it this time.

The doctor told me my uterus was too large to do a D&C on me right away. He sent me home to wait for two weeks and see if my uterus would go down in size to where they could safely perform a D&C. For anyone who doesn't know what a D&C is, it is where they put you out with a sedative and scrape the uterus out. I was truly terrified that I would pass the baby at home because I was so much further along this time. Nothing happened this time. I didn't have any labor pains, didn't pass anything, just some bleeding.

My stomach did go down some and I went back to the doctor two weeks later for my examination. The doctor said, "There is nothing there now so we won't be doing a D&C on you." I was shocked! I said, "What do you mean there is nothing there anymore? I didn't pass anything?" His standard answer for everything was, "Well sometimes nature just takes care of these things." All I could think was *what is going on here?* I was further along this time than I had ever been and I thought I felt the baby move or shift- but there was nothing there just two weeks later? I wondered, *Oh my God, what is going on?*

My husband and I bought our first house in Raytown, Missouri shortly after my last miscarriage. I still live in this house today forty-nine years later and will probably die here. Anyway, back to the pregnancies. I couldn't get pregnant and the doctor (after trying everything they had available at that time) decided to do corrective female surgery on me. He felt he just had to open me up to see what was going on with my female organs.

I had endometriosis, which is a buildup of tissue over the

ovaries in the tubes where the eggs come down. It was a major surgery, but I wanted a baby so, I had it. When they opened me, up my ovaries were totally embedded with tissue and my Fallopian tubes were lying along the side of my uterus instead of being next to the ovaries. No wonder I wasn't getting pregnant anymore. My uterus was tipped which he said was not that unusual to see but my uterus was grown to my back and that was very unusual. He said that was why I was not able to carry the babies very long, because my uterus couldn't expand because it was attached to my back.

I was in surgery for five hours as they cleaned off my ovaries and freed up my Fallopian tubes. They freed up my uterus too and sewed it to the wall in my abdomen. He told me he thought I would get pregnant now and I would be able to carry the baby full term.

So here my husband and I were with our new home and I had high hopes of having a child after my surgery and so many disappointments of the past. Well, it didn't happen. I never got pregnant again.

Finally, about a year later we decided to put in for adoption. We could have requested a boy or a girl but I decide to just wait and see what God gave us the same way as a couple would having their own. Unbelievable, but in nine months we got our baby and it was a boy! Without a doubt this was the happiest day of my life! I even felt it was more life changing than getting married. I was so happy and finally I felt complete for the first time in my life. I so strongly felt this was the child God wanted me to have, and I just had to go about it in a different way. This was my baby forever and I loved him with all my heart and I still do! My baby was special and I knew it. All of this about my son being so special will be explained in more detail later in the book.

"Alien abduction is cause of many miscarriages –
Aliens & Reptilians Steal Babies"

Stephenie Relfe B.Sc. Sydney

Chapter 8

The Spook Light Experience

I befriended a young woman whom with her husband rented my parents basement apartment when I was about 14 years old. We became fast friends, and she was about seven years older than me, so she could drive. We hung out a lot together, driving around the Drive-Ins and drinking cokes. Even after I got married we stayed friends and had a lot of fun together. Barbara and her husband came from the small town of Seneca, located just south of Joplin, MO.

Barbara was very homesick living here, and about ten years later they moved back to Seneca. We stayed in contact though, with letters and phone calls. My husband and I decided to take a trip to Seneca to visit and spend the weekend with them.

Barbara told me many stories about the Hornet Spook Light. The second night we were there, they took us out to see the Spook Light. In those days, I really hadn't heard all that much about the Spook Light, but it sounded interesting to me.

Barbara had a married sister and she and her husband went with us. Barbara drove and the three of us girls sat in the front seat and the three guys were in the back seat of this big old Chevy car. I think it was a '58 Chevy sedan which was good size with large bench seats in it. So we all drove out at about 10:00 p.m. and when we arrived at the location it was good and dark outside.

Having grown up in Seneca, they knew the best spot to park so we could see the Spook Light. This was near the intersection of E50 and State Line Road. There was an old broken down white shack there that had a sign (that was hanging sideways) saying **"Spook Light Museum."** Obviously, this place had been closed for a long time. The shack alone looked spooky to me with woods and vegetation grown up all over and around it. The museum was opened by Arthur Posie Meadows, known as "Spooky," after he spent several weeks camping in the area around 1940 and witnessed the light. He had heard stories about the light since childhood and wanted others to witness it, too. Visitors could view the light through a telescope for a quarter. Meadows and his museum became very well known in the mid-1950's with many newspapers spreading the story through articles, and as many as 200 people visited the museum and the area nightly hoping to see the mysterious light. Later, Arthur sold the museum to his brother-in-law Garland Middleton, who kept it running for many years until his death. The building was eventually destroyed by fire and is now gone.

The actual parking place was on the brink of a cliff, and we parked very close to the edge. We could see a very large field down below us (miles long & wide) that was flat and had some crops growing in it. Barbara said when they were kids, they would go on hayrides down there and the Spook Light would chase them!

There we all sat, waiting for the Spook Light. Barbara said not to talk above a whisper or it would not come near us. We were very quiet and just whispering or not saying anything at all. We must have sat there about twenty minutes, and sure enough we saw the light appear down below us in the field. It was a bright white light about the size of a beach ball, and it was just bouncing around in the field. Then, as if something drew it to us, it quit playing around in the field and was heading towards us!

We all got very quiet then as Barbara had warned us, "Don't make ANY sound and it will come to us." The Spook Light ended up right in front of the car and then it started coming up over the hood of the car. It was as if it were going to come in the car with us through the windshield!

It was only about a foot from reaching the windshield when all three of us girls started screaming at the top of our lungs. The light just quickly went up and totally disappeared! I thought my heart was going to stop. It was quite an experience. Now I keep wondering, what would have happened if we had not screamed? Would the light have come into the car? I think it would have because of the momentum it had and the way it was moving across the hood of the car. I also wonder- would it have hurt us?

I have never been back, but would love to go again just to see if it would react the same way. I know many people have studied the Hornet Spook Light and there are all kinds of theories as to what it may be from swamp gas, to headlights off the freeway. I truly don't think either one of those theories would cause a light to react the way this one did. It actually acted as if it had some intelligence or spirit about it. To seek us out the way it did and to react to our screams, well that sounds like an intelligence was controlling the object.

One of the things on my bucket list is to go back and try to find the Spook Light again.

Chapter 9

An Awakening and Psychic Events

I don't believe in coincidence. I think everything happens for a reason, and I have become more sure of this the older I get. I know there was something very strange about the way I had all those miscarriages. The entire time I lived in that basement, (where all my miscarriages happened) I felt watched. Even though my husband was there with me at night, I felt scared and had the strange sensation of being observed. I always knew in my gut that those miscarriages had some hidden meanings to them and they were not happening in a natural way. How did I know this? I have to say it was intuition that told there was more to the story than I was seeing at the time.

I started having psychic dreams, and they often came true. About seven years after my last miscarriage, I had a dream one night. Not just a dream, but one that I felt with everything in me really happened. I was sitting on a chrome bench just waiting for something. I didn't know what I was waiting for at the time. I was looking around at this unfamiliar place I was in and I didn't even know how I got to this room. I was just there. The space was large and round, with small windows that ran all the way around the room. The windows were about three feet above the chrome benches which also ran along the room, the windows were about two to three feet in height.

Everything in this room was shiny chrome which gave the room a bare and cold look, or maybe "sterile" would be a better word to describe it. There was an elevator or chrome doors to my left only about three feet from where I was sitting. Then to my right was this large machine type thing and the top of it was turning. This was all chrome, too. This machine looked similar to a luggage conveyer at an airport. It had chrome flaps overlaying each other that turned in one direction. (See the drawing.) I now think it could have been an anti-gravity machine. This machine was about 10-15 feet to my right so it was much further from me than the elevator doors.

I am sitting on the bench and the elevator doors open, and out walked a man with a child- a boy. The man was handsome with blond hair and he was tall. He wore a white robe and the child also had on a white robe. The robes were tied at the waist with gold colored ropes. The boy looked about seven years old, which coincided with the time when I had the last miscarriage. The man walked the child over to me. No one spoke a word at any time through this event. The man just kind of acted like he didn't know what to expect to happen next.

The boy had blond hair and blue eyes like mine, and very fine features. The man nudged the boy towards me. He stood right in front of me. I put my arms around him and held him so ever tightly for a long embrace that drew tears to my eyes. The child seemed shy, but hugged me back. I knew without a doubt this was my child I was holding! It didn't last but a few minutes. The tall man took the boy by the shoulder and walked him back to the elevator or doors. I saw the boy look at me as he was pulled away as if he didn't want to leave me, but he went quietly with the man.

This was a very upsetting dream for me. I knew I had seen

my child and he was alive and well, but I had such trouble understanding why I had this dream. I had my own son now who answered all my desires of being a mother. It was just so real and so strange I'll never forget it.

About eight years after that "dream" I bought a book on a whim. It was about aliens, flying saucers, and abductions. I can remember reading this book so vividly – I was in my living room in the afternoon by myself.

I was reading about a woman who claimed to have a series of miscarriages, only this lady could remember being abducted by the aliens. She remembered them taking her babies out of her at about three months of pregnancy. That's the same time when I would always lose my babies. This woman said they took her up to the space ship years later and brought her child to her. Her child was half alien and half human, otherwise known as a hybrid.

She said the aliens did this because they wanted the hybrid children to have some connection with their human parent. They also felt it helped the children to know where they came from and to meet their mother. This woman went on to describe how she was taken to an all- chrome round room to meet her child. I about fell off the couch reading this - and what an epiphany I had, this was exactly what had happened to me!

Many things started to fall into place. Things I had wondered about for so many years. It was all beginning to make some sense to me. I can't remember the actual abductions, but this would sure explain the terror of being taken all through my childhood. It would explain many of the strange things that happened.

Now I believe that scary face I saw looking at me in my crib was an alien. That is why as an infant, I remember it happening so vividly. They knew from the time I was an infant they were going to use me as a baby producer. For what reason I was chosen, I do not know. Although, I have heard that often this phenomenon will run in families. Its seems the aliens may want to stick with certain blood lines for abduction and reproduction. Would aliens follow certain blood lines because of the DNA that runs in families? Maybe my parents and/or grandparents were abducted at some point of their lives? Perhaps that was why my great-grandmother Nettie had the gift of being so psychic.

I have pondered many possibilities as to why whoever or whatever is responsible chose me. These experiences prompted me to do a lot of research about aliens and abductions to try to figure things out. So many things fit with my own experiences that I am sure now that I had been abducted many times as a child. The scar on my stomach, the fear I had of being taken, the spaceman-looking creature following me, and the miscarriages and dreams were all seemingly related. And yet today strange things keep happening. The list continues. I think the extraterrestrials messed my female organs up so badly from being abducted all those years and at such a young age that I was never able to have a child. God only knows what they did to me. I am resentful towards them for taking my babies! I am resentful for them making me and my brother grow up in fear, too.

I have heard men say that aliens have taken sperm from them for reproduction purposes. Then years later they would be abducted and taken aboard a space craft to meet up with their offspring, which were usually hybrids. So it is apparent that these occurrences happen not only to females, but with men, too.

My brother, Ted, had a similar thing happen to him. When Ted was in his early twenties he was living with his girlfriend, who is now his wife. My mother had moved six blocks from me in Raytown, after she and dad got a divorce. Mom called Ted one day and said, "I am scared. Something keeps turning on the motion detector lights in the backyard and the dogs start barking." Mom said this had been happening for several nights and she thought someone was snooping around the yard. She asked him to come over and spend the night with her, so he did.

Ted said they went to bed that night and he went right to sleep. Ted heard mom leave early the next morning for work and then fell back to sleep. He said he woke up but he couldn't move or speak, it was as if he was paralyzed. He said he saw a gray alien standing next to him and it had a tube-like instrument that the alien slid over his penis. The alien took the tube and Ted watched it walk into the other bedroom with the tube which was full of sperm. Mom's house was very small and only had the two bedrooms which were very close together. It still seems strange that the alien walked into the other bedroom and not out the back door. Mom's bedroom faced the street and I don't understand why it would go that way, but maybe it just didn't make any difference.

Ted was totally unable to move or speak and the next thing he knew, he was asleep again. Did he have a dream? I don't think so. It totally fits the profile of how these aliens

operated when doing abductions. They can paralyze us and

do whatever they want to us. They have the power to wipe things out of our minds, as if our minds were blackboards and they erase the parts they don't want us to remember. I have no recollection of being abducted, yet all the signs are there and I know in my heart I was abducted. What I have are bits and pieces of a puzzle and I am beginning to put a lot of the pieces of the puzzle together. I know what they did to me and my brother our entire lives.

This happening with Ted also makes me believe my mother was being abducted too. That's why her light detectors were going off and she was so scared. My mom told Ted that this had been happening for a while and she was concerned about what was going on at her house.

My mother had numerous experience with psychic abilities throughout her lifetime. One day mom told me she knew her husband (my stepfather), Bill was dying. She said she woke up in the middle of the night and happened to look up at the lamp next to her bed. On the lamp shade, she saw Jesus and Jesus was hanging his head and looking very sad. She said, "I think he was telling me that this was going to end badly. He just looked so very sad." Shortly after, Bill became terminally ill with cancer. She was so right. Bill found out he had cancer and he was in the later stages. One night we had to take him to the hospital. He was very sick and was throwing up blood. They sent him home as they couldn't do much for him. He had esophageal cancer which had spread to his stomach. The next morning, he got up, took his gun and went out to the patio where he shot himself in the head. My mother was still inside the house at the time. It just destroyed my mother, and she only lived about five years longer, never getting over his tragic death. Mom knew for sure at that point why Jesus was looking so sad in the vision she had of him.

Another story I want to share is about my beloved grandmother, Effie, who passed away from a stroke that killed her instantly. I had never lost anyone that I was so close to before and losing her was devastating. I was in my late 20's and I was so close to her and grandpa because I practically lived with them as a child. Never have I been crushed so badly as when I lost her. Even though I did know she was getting very old, I couldn't imagine life without her. She had been my second mother all my life and I only felt pure love coming from her.

Grandma Effie never smoked until she got into her forties and then she became a chain smoker when she got into her eighties. My mom and I cleaned up her house after her death because we knew people and relatives would be coming over to visit us and grandpa. Grandpa did not smoke any longer- he smoked in his younger days but quit a long time ago. My mom went to see grandpa the next day and when she walked into the dining room she found a couple of burned up cigarette butts laying on the buffet. Mom and I had just cleaned up all the butts off the buffet the day before as well as the ones grandma had let burn out on her bedroom dresser.

Grandma did this often in her old age. She would forget she had a lit cigarette and just walk out of the room leaving it to burn out on the furniture. It's a wonder she never burned the house down. Then mom found some other burned up cigarettes in grandma's bedroom on her dresser.

Mom called me and asked me to come over. Her voice was shaky, so I could tell something was up with her. I arrived there quickly and she showed me the burned cigarette butts.

We just looked at each other as if to say "What the hell?" We knew we had cleaned all the butts up, so where did they come from? Mom looked at me and said, "I don't think she knows she is dead yet and she has been back here." I totally agreed with my mother as it made the most sense for what we had found. After the first week of her death, this never happened again. Either she didn't know she was dead or she was letting us know that she was still around us. I am hoping for the latter scenario!

"Human kind gradually begins to remove the blinders from their consciousness about life, about what is real and what is not. Intuition and psychic abilities increase."

Elaine Seller, You Multi-Dimensional Work book: Exercises for Energetic Awakening

Chapter 10

Psychic Dreams

As my husband and I settled into our new house we started having strange phenomena happen. At that time, we had a single garage and the door to the garage was right off the kitchen. Once you stepped out into the garage you could go down the basement steps to the left or to the right where there was a door that led outside. The door leading from the kitchen to the garage was just a wooden door with three panes of square glass, so half the door was glass. The door had a lock in the handle and at night before going to bed I always checked the door to be sure it was locked.

I always headed straight for the kitchen upon rising to start the coffee, and to my surprise I would often find the door opened about four to five inches! I would accuse my husband of being up sometime in the night and opening the door. He would say, "You've got to be kidding me, why on Earth would I do something so crazy? I would tell you if I was up and left the door open." This was true. What point would there be to something so silly? I just couldn't figure it out and there was only the two of us in the house. At night it became a big deal for both of us to check the door to make sure it was closed and locked. Damn if we wouldn't get up and that darn door would be open about a foot! It was as if something was just defying us and opening the door to prove it could do it.

This really started to drive me crazy and I could not figure out how that door would open when it was locked. Any person doing that would have to break into the garage or basement first to get to the kitchen door. I had a big dog back then and he was very protective of me, and if anyone was coming in the house he would have barked and awakened us. I kept pondering about how this was happening and could not figure it out. Getting tired of this situation, I went to the hardware store one day and bought a sliding bolt lock. That night I had my husband put it on the door about four inches off the floor at the base of the door. That way, even if someone broke the glass out of the door they would not have been able to reach the bolt.

I wasn't feeling safe getting up and finding a locked door standing open so I sure hoped this would stop it. I figured if it was a ghost turning a door handle to unlock a door that would be much easier than unsnapping the bolt and sliding it open. I was right. I don't know what or who was opening that door but the bolt stopped it. I never found that door open again after locking the bolt. I still wonder if it may have been a ghost or extraterrestrials.

One evening my husband and I had quarreled. It was nothing real serious, but I got very mad at him. He went to bed before me and I was still watching television in the living room. About 20 minutes later, he started yelling, "Jean, get in here, now." Then he yelled again "Come to bed right now!" I finally went into the bedroom and said "Why do you want me to come to bed right now?" He said, "Well, as soon I laid down in bed something started shaking the bed. I mean, really shaking this bed! I think it's because something is mad at me for fighting with you!" I said, "You mean something like a ghost?" He answered, "Yes, I don't know any other way to explain it!" I went to bed and sure enough the bed did not shake again.

I had a rocker love seat that was in the corner of the living room. Numerous times when I would be home alone that rocker would just start rocking! There was no one home but me, and no breeze, but there was no logical explanation for why or how it could be rocking. It would just creep me out every time it happened. It was one of those things that just stood the hair up on the back of my neck. The only thing I could think of was perhaps it was great grandma Nettie because she always loved sitting in her rocking chair and perhaps she was visiting me. I figured if anyone could come back as a spirit, it was her.

I would see dark things in my kitchen and they would dart around. I couldn't see them if I looked right at them, but would see these objects from my peripheral vision. My kitchen, dining room, and living room are all open where you can see from one room into the other. I would sit on my sofa in the living room watching TV and saw dark things moving around in the kitchen. They looked like humanoid shadows as they darted around the kitchen.

Several times I saw dark objects moving through my hallway by the bedrooms. This too would cause the hair on my arms to rise. Numerous times I had something touch me on the butt or down on my upper thigh, like a pat. I felt that it was a male entity. After about five years or so, it just stopped! I hadn't seen shadows in my house for many years until lately, and I will tell you about that later- but they are back!

My husband was in heavy construction building bridges so he was working on the highways. Sometimes my husband's job was to be the flagman that stops the cars on the highway and then let them pass. This was a very dangerous job, being a flagman on some of those busy highways. One night, I had a vision dream. It was one of those dreams that was just too real to be only a dream. In this dream, I saw an accident that happened on the highway. I could see a black car on its side on the highway. It was a very bad car accident and I could smell gasoline so strong, it was as if someone was holding a gas can under my nose! I kept screaming out, "Get away from that car! It's going to blow up! Smell the gasoline, it's going to blow!"

The next morning, I woke up and was having coffee with my husband. I told him about the dream that I had and I warned him to be careful on his job. A few days later he came home from work and told me there had been a wreck on the highway where he was working. He said one of the cars had rolled over on its side and a man was still in it. My husband and a couple of other construction workers grabbed the man and pulled him to safety. He said just after they walked away from the wrecked car, it blew up. He told me when they were trying to get the guy out of the car, there was a strong smell of gas! Was it a coincidence that I had that dream and this wreck happened shortly afterward?

I seemed to pick up most future events in relation to my husband in my dreams for some reason. Sometime later, maybe a year or so, I had another vision dream. In this dream, as I call them "real dreams", I again could see a busy highway. I could hear people yelling and I knew something bad had happened. Then I could see lots of blood all over the highway. It was a frightening dream and I woke up in a sweat. I was terrified!

The next morning, I told my husband what I had seen in my dream. As I recall he didn't pay a lot of attention to this or what I was telling him. Just a few days later he came home and told me, "Oh My God, we had a terrible accident at work today." My husband was on one end of the construction zone flagging traffic and there was another man at the other end flagging traffic. Someone had come through the construction zone at a very high rate of speed and hit the other flagman. My husband said, the vehicle just tore that guy to pieces and there was blood everywhere. I knew he was right because I had seen it in my dream.

Not too many months later I had another dream about my husband. He was a scrappy type of guy, he worked construction and he sometimes had a bad temper, so this dream wasn't much of a shock to me. It seemed true to form for him. I dreamed he got into a fist fight with another man on his job. This other guy was short, but very stocky and he hit my husband in the mouth. I could see blood dripping off my husband's mouth and down his chin. I told him about my dream the next morning about my dream and we laughed about it.

That very night he came home from work and told me that he and one of his construction buddies were just messing around throwing punches at each other. Yes, the other guy hit him in the mouth, but accidentally. And my husband got a bloody mouth from it! He said to me, "You need to stop having dreams about me. This crap is getting old," and we laughed about it!

Years later I had one of my "real dreams" but at the time it didn't make a lot sense to me. This dream scared the hell out of me. It was as if I was watching a movie. I saw a man get disemboweled! It was terrible, and I was horrified at having this dream. I couldn't tell how it happened or who the man was but it was bloody and frightening. It was as if I was watching it happening and I could hear other people yelling saying, "Oh my God, he has been disemboweled!"

My first husband was working on a new bridge here in Kansas City over the Missouri River. He was standing on a barge that had a rope tied to a tug boat. The tug boat was pulling the barge with the rope and the rope broke loose from the tug boat. This caused the taunt rope with a metal bar attached to fly back at the barge and the metal bar hit my ex-husband in the gut, disemboweling him!

His brother was on the barge working with him and ran over and tried to hold his bowels inside him. They said my ex-husband never lost consciousness through this and they got him to the hospital. Nothing but a miracle saved him. He was one tough man to survive what he did. He is still alive today, but how, I don't know.

When I got over the shock of what had happened, I remembered my dream. That's what that dream was telling me. I always had that connection with my ex-husband, knowing when something was going to happen to him. I doubt that I have that now as we have been apart for about 40 years. I really don't want to know about these kinds of things happening unless I can do something in time to prevent them. But I have no control over my dreams and I don't always understand them completely. I can usually tell the difference now when I have a normal dream and what is one of my "real dreams". This is something I am still working on- getting psychic messages that are sometimes in dreams, and sometimes in other ways.

"Dreams may contain ineluctable truths, philosophical pronouncements, illusions, wild fantasies, memories, plans, anticipation, irrational experiences, even telepathic vision, and heaven know what besides."

Carl Jung

Chapter 11

Some Tragic Years

I think most people have gone through some years that bad things just seem to happen to them. Sometimes it is one bad thing right after another. I was 29 years old when I met Chet and we were married a year later. My dad had moved from our family home on Crysler in Independence, to a farm that was right along I-70 in Sweet Springs, Missouri. It was 60 miles from Independence and took a little over an hour to drive there from my house in Raytown. Dad bought 100 acres of farmland with an old farm house on it. He built his dream there of having a small airport. He made a grass field runway with a metal barn building he used as a hangar. My dad lived to be flying- he just loved it and everything about having his own airport. He had a large billboard put up outside the hangar that read, "Ted's Flying Field".

He started getting the attention of a lot of pilots that would fly out to his field and they would just sit in the hangar talking planes. Oh, how he relished this fun! He had lots of pilot friends and he spent hours working on his planes. He usually had small Cessna's and Piper Cubs that he would fly. He thought he was a barnstormer like the Red Baron and loved to buzz some his friends' barns even to the point of running the airplanes wheels across the tops of the metal roofs. He was finally living his dream of owning his own airport and flying his planes.

Dad got really carried away with this thought of barnstorming and wanted to get a biplane. He bought a home-built biplane which was called a Fly Baby, and was learning to taxi it out on his runway. They had built up the grass runway with dirt to get the runway leveled out, so on both sides of the runway there were very deep ditches and they would fill up with water when it rained. At the end of the runway was a creek, so the pilot sure wanted to be airborne before reaching the creek. When you get into an open cockpit biplane you wear a harness that has hooks on it that attach to the inside of the plane.

Dad told me that these biplanes had very touchy rudders. The rudder pedals are used to steer the plane like a steering wheel. This is because the lines that are connected to the rudders are very short and this makes the pedals very touchy in a little biplane. So he took off in his Fly Baby biplane, taxied down the runway, and he flipped the plane. The plane landed upside down straddling the ditch on the side of the runway. Dad was strapped in with the harness upside down with his nose about 1 inch from the deep water in the ditches! Thank heaven there were several other pilots around and they all ran to help him, and they flipped the plane back over to get him out.

Dad did eventually fly that plane, but for only short distances. He was really spooked by this plane but wanted to continue to learn to fly these open cockpit biplanes. He lived with his Trade-A-Plane magazine always with him and always shopping, buying, or trading planes. He found another kit biplane called a Pete-In-Pole that was built in Minnesota. He drove up North to Minnesota to look at the plane and then bought it. He hauled it back to Sweet Springs, Missouri on a flatbed truck.

The plane needed some work on it so Dad had a young 33-year-old pilot friend who lived on the farm across the highway help him out. This young man would often help Dad and they enjoyed flying together. My brother, Teddy, was visiting my dad one day and looked at this new biplane. He said, "Wow Dad, I would love to go up with you in this plane." Teddy told me Dad just quickly turned to him saying, "You will never go up with me in this plane! This plane isn't safe for two people to fly in because the prop does not cut into the air enough to carry two people. There were two seats in the plane so Teddy didn't understand this. Teddy said Dad about took his head off yelling at him about how he was not going to be riding in this plane until he got a new prop for it and knew it was safe to ride in. This didn't seem to Teddy to be a normal reaction from Dad.

A few weeks later my dad and his pilot neighbor were working on my dad's plane. They decided they needed to fly over to Marshall Airport to buy some parts they needed for the plane. My dad had never changed the prop on that plane even after what he told my brother previously. They got into the plane and took off. My dad had a hired hand who helped him out around the farm and Dad said to him, "Well you are probably going to see us get killed trying to fly this plane. But we are going over to the Marshall airport to buy some parts."

The worker stood there and watched them take off. He said Dad only had about 150 feet altitude when the nose of the plane went straight down into a dive. Per the worker, Dad just didn't have enough altitude to pull the plane out of the dive, but just before the plane crashed, Dad was starting to get the nose up. Dad was killed immediately and the younger guy lived for 3 months then died from his injuries. They told me that every bone in my dad's body was broken.

The shock of knowing he was okay one minute and gone the

next was very overwhelming. I was in a bad state for about a year before I came out of it. When my brother first heard the news he was running up and down his driveway, holding his head and screaming over and over, "I want my Sis, where's my Sis?" My mother called me and said, "Jean, your brother is losing it and he is screaming for you. Get down there now." I got to my brother's house and we just held on to each other crying and in shock. Then there was grandmother, Nellie. My dad was her only child, so my brother and I had to break the news to her. It was just terrible. Still today I can't believe that my father, an experienced pilot, crashed that plane.

About three years previously, I married a man named Chet. He was a police detective at the time I met him, and he later became the manager of several fitness centers. We were married for six years when he died of lung cancer at the early age of 46. He was almost 10 years older than me, so I was a young, 36-year-old widow. I had lost the two most important men in my life within two years of each other. Both died a tragic death, and it was way too soon for both of them to go. I collected social security for myself and my young son Tommy, who was 12 at the time. I was working in a bank making very little money, way less than the social security was paying me, so I took this opportunity to go to college and worked part time while raising Tommy.

At first I didn't know what I wanted to do with my life, but after attending college for a while I decided I wanted to be a teacher. College opened my eyes to so many things that I had been ignorant of- it was like the world opened up for me. I decided I wanted to do that for children- to try to open the world for them and teach them how to survive this world. An education doesn't make you smarter per say, what it does is it gives you more opportunities in life. An education enables you to have choices in life that you wouldn't have otherwise. I learned from working so many menial jobs for little pay, I wanted to do better things with my life and working with children seemed to be it.

I found that when I took science classes I excelled in them, and I loved learning science. I think this was because science helped to explain so many things about the world and beyond. Within nine years of starting college, I had my Masters in Education and I was teaching middle school science. I taught school for about twenty years and then retired. Now I still substitute teach to stay active in teaching, but without the full responsibility, which works well for me!

"There is a saying in Tibetan, "Tragedy should be utilized as a source of strength. No matter what sort of difficulties, how painful experience is, if we lose our hope, that's our real disaster."

Dalai Lama

Chapter 12

Repetitive Dreams

I have only had two repetitive dreams in my life. The first one started when I was about twenty years old and continued through my early thirties. I would dream about a bridge that was just a few blocks from my grandparent's house on Maywood in Independence. I would be with about ten to fifteen other people in total. We were all frightened to death. We were inside a room inside a bridge. I even knew which bridge it was as it was the next street to the west from my grandparent's house. We would run from one side of the bridge (room) to other the side of the bridge (room). I remember how everyone was so terrified! We would yell and scream and keep running from one side of the bridge to the other in great fear!

I had this dream many times and it made no sense to me at all. Why would a group of people that I didn't know and me run from one end of the inside of this bridge to the other? All the time, we were screaming and in great fear. I could feel my heart racing and I was so frightened as I ran from one side to the other. I thought "How do you get inside a concrete bridge?" I kept having this dream over and over. It came to me today- that was no bridge in my dream. It was a rectangular room with no windows, and I was in there like the others frightened out of our wits! But scared of what? I know now, it came to me great clarity as I write this book. I think the writing process jarred my mind into remembering.

We were all captives of ET's and being held there until they were ready for their next victim! That is why we kept running back and forth to each end of the room. I think they were coming after us from doors at each end of the room, so if a door opened we all ran to the other end, hoping to escape our torturers! The bridge was a ship that the aliens were on and they took us there to do whatever they were going to do.

As I look back on this I don't think these were dreams I was having, I think it was really happening to me and I just remembered it as a dream. Not until today, when I started to remember what really happened did I see the reality of the experience. I could hardly wait to get it down on paper. I think "they" have certain victims they pick up on a regular basis and I was one of them. Guess I was one of the lucky ones ever since I was in the crib and they chose me to abduct. Another strange thing is I was living at my grandparent's house when I was in the crib. The bridge (or room) I was in during my dream was in my grandparent's neighborhood. I spent a lot of my time while growing up at my grandparent's house, so I think they were taking me from there and the house on Crysler street. They seemed to always know where I was and where to find me.

At the young age of thirty I had a complete hysterectomy, which means they took out *all* my female organs. I suffered for so many years with pain and bleeding just in hopes of having a child. However, at twenty-four, I adopted my precious baby boy and there was no reason for me suffer through any more physical pain. I stopped having this dream about the same time I had the hysterectomy. Was that a coincidence? I think not.

I still feel they have taken me since my hysterectomy, but

many times I don't think they are putting me through the torture they did before with the babies. I am not sure why I feel this way, but I think I am right. I am so pleased to know I finally figured out that crazy dream that always stayed with me! They are still doing experiments on me because I wake up with just too many injuries such as needle holes, bruises, and red marks that a normal person doesn't get while they are sleeping. I think they have put many implants in me for who knows what reason, but I am hoping sometimes they do things that will help me with my health.

There is another reoccurring dream I have had. It started about a year after my father's death. I kept dreaming dad was talking to me mentally, but not physically face to face. Dad kept telling me to go to grandma Nellie's house and get into her "Fibber McGee" closet, the dead-end stairway that grandma used for storage. I told grandma about my dream and I asked her if my dad had anything stored in that closet. When dad had moved from the Crysler house to Sweet Springs he stored some stuff at grandma's house, but she said it was all stored in her basement.

Grandma would always insist that my dad never stored anything in that closet. We called it a closet because grandmother had a door put up on it that would latch. However, I continued to have the dream.

Finally, one day I was visiting my grandma and I thought about it again. I said, "Grandma, I know you say dad never put any of his things in this closet but do mind if I just look through it?" She said, "Oh, no child, go right ahead and look." I remember there was a small window inside the stairway on the first landing that let a lot of light in that day.

I was pilfering through all stuff in the closet. Right where the window was located on the landing if you turned to the right there were about five more steps before the wall where it dead-ended. When I got up to the top steps, I found an old cigar box. The cigar box had my dad's name on it. The box was filled with a few photographs and some personal papers of his. I took the box downstairs and the two of us sat down at her kitchen table. We began looking at the stuff and there were pictures that I am sure my dad wanted me to throw away, and I did. But among the paperwork was a pregnancy test result that my dad's mistress had taken, and my dad had kept it in the box.

I knew many years back, that my dad had an affair with a lady, who along with her husband, rented our basement apartment. She had two little girls, and when the kids left for school my dad would go downstairs to be with Diane. My dad worked the second shift for years and my mother worked days so he was free during the days to do whatever he wanted. This pregnancy test was in Diane's name stating she had a positive pregnancy test and my dad had kept it. It had to have meant something to him or he would have never kept that paperwork through all those years.

Diane and her husband moved out after Diane got pregnant. They did keep in touch though, because my mom knew where they lived somewhere in Independence. Evidently, my mom knew what was going on and just didn't care that much about the affair or my dad. One evening, my mother looked at me and said, "Let's go see Diane and Walt's new baby. I want to see if it looks like your dad." I was speechless. Did mom really say that to me?

I had caught my dad down there with Diane a couple of times and I knew how he was about chasing women, but I didn't know that mom knew about it. Mom and I didn't say anything to each other- we just drove over there and saw the baby. Mom just greeted Diane like they were the best of friends. The baby was a boy, and his name was Vincent. We left after a short visit and I remember riding home with mom. Mom never said anything during the drive, so after a while I had to ask her, "Well, do you think the baby looked like dad?" Mom just calmly said, "No, I don't think it looked anything like him." I was relieved to hear her say that but was still in shock that she thought it could have been my dad's child.

Now what? I was in shock with all the stuff I found in the cigar box. My mind was racing and all I could think was that I must have a half-brother somewhere. My grandma was just looking at me (maybe she was in shock too) and she said, "Please Jean, let's just throw all this stuff away. I am sure that is why your dad wanted you to find it." So I did just that. I threw it all outside into the trash bin.

After having years to think about this though, I wish I had kept the pregnancy test because I think grandma was dead wrong. I think the reason my dad wanted me to find this stuff was so I would know I had a half-brother. I am just sure of that now. The bad part is that I cannot remember Diane or Walt's last name, nor can my brother. I do remember that they moved to New York State, but that's all I can remember. The reason I mention their name is maybe this book will someday reach Vincent and he will figure it out. Stranger things have happened- but it's my only hope of finding him. I have had the thought that I could get hypnotized to remember their last name, if it would work. After I found this stuff the dream stopped, so the repetitiveness of Dad causing me to have that dream was fulfilled.

A Warning Dream

This dream was not repetitive, but I feel it is well worth mentioning. After my mother got her divorce from my dad, she rented a house not far from me and my brother lived with her.

One night, I had a dream that while mother was at this rented house, she opened the kitchen door to the garage. There stood this menacing looking man and he was grinning at her like "I am going to get you and kill you!" He had rotten yellow teeth with a gold tooth in the front that was shining. He was short and burly chested, and he looked very strong and very mean. He had short hair like a burr cut that was greasy and dirty looking, and his clothes looked dirty, too. I knew he meant to kill her and I was terrified! In my dream, my mother just stood there and stared at him in fright, unable to move. Then I woke up, but after having such a frightening dream as that, I couldn't forget it because it seemed so real.

I debated for a few days whether to tell my mom about the dream. Then I decided maybe this was a warning and I should tell her so she could be aware of what was going on around her. I told my mother about the dream with all the terrible details. Mom just looked at me and said, "Damn Jean, I had that very same dream and saw that very man in my dream!" She said she saw the gold tooth and all of it like I had described to her. We had both had the same dream within a few days of each other and all the details of him being in the garage and physical description were the same.

This really shook both of us. What did it mean? How could we both have had the same dream? Stranger yet, it never happened, thank the Lord! So what was the purpose of this dream? My mother moved from that house a few months later and bought a house six blocks from mine. Maybe that is why it never happened and it was a warning for her to leave that rental house!

"The repetitive patterns in your dream reveal some of the most valuable information about yourself. It may point to a conflict, situation or matter in your waking life that remains unresolved or unsettled. Some urgent underlying message in your unconscious is demanding to be understood."

www.dreammoods.com

Jean Walker

Chapter 13

Weird Happenings

When my brother was in his early fifties, he went fishing one warm and sunny day during the summer at Longview Lake in Lee's Summit, Missouri. He was fishing below the dam area, and there were two other men across the lake area from him fishing as well. Ted said the two other men were not together and but they were both on the east side of the water and he was on the west side, fishing.

To the north of where Ted was fishing was a wooded area. Ted said he was just sitting in a lawn chair watching his bobber and hoping for a fish to strike when he noticed an object that appeared over his head. He said it looked very dark, a lot like a cloud, but he didn't think it was a cloud as it was so low in the sky. A few minutes later a young couple came walking out of the woods on the north side. They walked up the west side of the bank where my brother was fishing. Ted said they were only a couple of hundred feet from him and he could see them well.

Ted said he looked over at them and the young man had pointed ears like Spock on Star Trek. He said both the male and female had little tiny noses, and their overall appearance was very much like pixies, only they were normal in height like an average adult. He said they appeared to be about 17 to 22 years old but they just had a very strange look about them, and were not quite normal.

The male just dropped his blue jeans down to his ankles and laid down on the bank. Ted said it was obvious that he had an erection but his penis was shaped very weirdly. The blond girl then dropped her jeans and sat down on the guy, only she was facing away from the guy's face, they were both facing towards the east.

Ted said he didn't know what the hell to do, so he just sat there watching his fishing line in disbelief. Ted looked over at the other two men fishing across from him and he said one guy kind of looked over at the couple for just a few seconds but acted like nothing unusual was happening. He said the other man never looked at the couple in any way that he could tell. Ted said he just sort of tried to keep an eye on what was going on with this couple from the corner of his eye without looking directly at them anymore.

Ted said after a few minutes the couple stopped having

sex, got up and pulled their jeans back up. Then the young man walked over to Ted and stopped when he got about three feet from Ted's face. Ted said the guy just leaned over and stared at Ted in the face! Ted said, "I just ignored him. I just didn't acknowledge his presence at all." After about a minute the guy walked back to the girl and two of them just walked back into the woods.

Neither of us can figure this one out. I think it has to go under the "Strange but true" category! If anyone reading this has had a similar experience or thinks they can explain this strange pixie looking couple having sex in the daylight at a public lake, please let me know. Were they extraterrestrials? There was that strange dark thing right over his head, which may have been a UFO.

Editor's note: A large number of strange incidents involving UFOs have been reported at this lake and others nearby.

Ted had another weird experience happen to him. This happened in October of 2014 at the Truman Library in Independence, Missouri. Ted, in addition to his full- time job, worked part-time for Truman Library as a custodian for 16 years to supplement his income. One Saturday, he walked into the main auditorium at the end of day, around 4:30 pm. The library would show films in the auditorium about Harry Truman's life. Ted walked down the rows of chairs towards the stage to see if there was any trash on the floor. He then turned and walked back to front of the auditorium. He was alone in the auditorium.

As he was walking towards the front of the auditorium he looked up at the projection booth to see if anyone was there, but it was empty since it was closing time. He was looking in between the rows of chairs after reaching the back rows.

There he saw this apparition appear that was about 15 feet in front of him. This apparition was unlike anything he had ever seen before in his life. The entire object was radiating in brilliant hyper colors of light that looked like crystals. It was much like the shape of a snowflake only very large.

The top of the object looked like a whisk broom with crystal spikes about 10 to 15 inches in length sticking out of it. The middle section of the object was a square shape that had things that looked like flower petals 3 inches across in layers that would flip over and over and ran down center of it. The entire object was giving off colors that were brilliant. He had never seen such beautiful colors. They were mostly emerald green with a pinkish red, and a metallic blue, with gold and silver colors mixed in to it. He described it as the strangest and most beautiful thing he had ever seen. The object had crystal spikes that stuck out all the way around it emitting lights. Ted said the apparition had a mist of tiny water droplets all around it looking like a fog that was emitting light.

The bottom of the object tapered to a "V", ending in a point. Ted said the object was also transparent and he could see everything through the apparition. Then this apparition started moving towards him. He said it was moving at the speed that a grown man would walk but for some strange reason he was not afraid of it. The object floated up to him and went right into him!

He said he turned around and looked behind him to see if it had gone through him but nothing was there. The apparition had gone into him and stayed there! He said the only thing he felt was a kind of whoosh of air that went over him when it entered him. Ted had no ill feelings or bad effects from it except for the mystery of what object was and why it went into him.

Ted was asking me what I thought this could have been, but I had no answers for him as I have never heard of anything like this before. So I called my friend, Margie Kay, and told her about it. I asked her if she had any idea of what this object was and what it doing. She told me, "Yes, I have heard of these apparitions before, and it is a good thing. This usually happens to good people and this was most likely something divine with a high vibration that would be there to assist Ted." My brother has always been a very good person and deeply into the spirit of God, so I felt this was a good explanation of what had happened to him. That was hy this apparition was beautiful as it was a divine, spiritual being. See drawing on the next page.

Ted lives in Blue Springs Missouri in a new home. One day in 2008, he got up at about 2:00 am to let his dog outside. While he was standing on his patio waiting on his dog, he looked up and just ten feet above the roof top he saw a bright blue ball of light come sailing over his house at a very slow speed. He said it was about the size of a basketball and deep blue in color. It flew over his house, then flew over his neighbor's house without stopping and just disappeared out of sight.

Ted said he could not figure out what the heck the object was or what it was doing. I think it could have been an *extraterrestrial drone* (since Ted and I have been abducted) checking things or him out. I find it strange that it found Ted outside at that hour. Was it something spiritual in nature and looking for Ted? What was it up to? What did it want? What was it? So many possibilities. It could also have been a drone from our own military and it was spying on people.

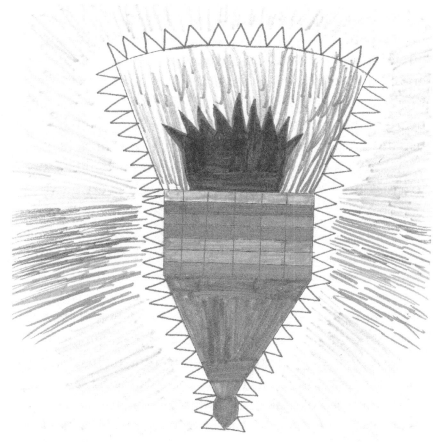

Apparition at the Harry S. Truman Library Auditorium

Ted has also seen other strange things at his home. He witnessed two amber orbs inside the house going through the hallways and out the walls. These orbs could be ET's or spirits, but I lean more towards the ET's. Again, the ET's could be checking him out or taking him and he just doesn't remember being taken. He has also experienced shadows being cast on his block windows in the bathroom and something beating on the side of the house in the middle of the night.

Chapter 14

Other UFO Sightings

In 1980 my brother was working for some family friends of ours, Wayne and Bettie. Bettie had grown up with our mother and we had known them all of our lives. They had bought an old farm house not too far from us and Wayne was remodeling it. Ted would help Wayne, doing everything from plumbing, putting in new windows, painting, yard work, and whatever needed to be done.

On one October fall evening at about twilight, Ted and Wayne were in the upstairs bedroom of this house putting in a new window. There was a horse farm right across the street from Wayne's house and Ted just happened to look out that direction to see some very strange lights. Ted told Wayne, "Look at this, Wayne. What the hell is that?" The two men stood there and watched what looked like a UFO flying just above the treetops.

Ted said they just stood there in amazement watching this thing. Ted described the UFO as having a brass colored bottom with a chrome top and there were heat waves coming off the bottom of this craft. Ted thinks the dome shaped craft was about 18 -20 feet across. The UFO hovered about ten feet above the trees as they watched it for a couple of minutes. Then the craft flew to the east for a few seconds and appeared to be landing behind the trees in a pasture area.

By the time Ted left Wayne's house, which was about 45 minutes later, it was dark. Ted said on his way home he drove past the general area where he thought the UFO had landed but saw nothing. He said, "Really Sis, I was so shaken over seeing that thing, I didn't look too hard for it, but I caught no sight of it or any strange lights in the fields." Ted felt it must have taken off again during the time he was preparing to leave Wayne's house.

Ted's recent sighting: Ted was working in eastern Independence, Missouri at a large factory. One morning, Ted was arriving to work and he was running late, so everyone else was already in the building. This was in the fall of the year and in the early morning it was still dark. Ted saw a UFO hovering over the plant and it had a saucer shape to it about 30 feet in diameter. It was right after spotting the UFO that the saucer started lifting up very slowly and traveled towards the east at about five mph.

Ted was already late so he couldn't stand there and watch it any longer. After entering the building, Ted ran up steps as fast as he could to look out the windows. By the time Ted had reached the second floor and looked out to where he had seen the UFO, it was gone. He was very disappointed that nobody else had seen the saucer. He then talked with some of the other workers, but could not find anyone else who had seen it. *Editor's note: This location is the site of multiple credible UFO sightings since the 1960's.*

Jean's sighting: I remarried several years after Chet's death. I married a man I had been friends with for many years. Richard worked as a special agent for the department of defense, was a former police detective, and a pilot/instructor. Richard and I had gone to McDonalds one evening (right after dark) and were picking up our order at the drive through window. I was in the passenger seat when something caught my eye out my window to my right. Looking to the south, I saw about five or six large, white glowing balls or saucer shaped lights that appeared to be objects. These objects were bright white lights. They were coming at a slanted position as if for a landing. They were in a formation pattern coming in with the largest one landing first and the others following. They appeared to be landing about five to ten miles from where we were at sitting at McDonalds.

When I first saw the objects, I yelled at Richard, "Look, look at that!" Richard saw them too, and we both just stared at them in amazement. We couldn't believe what we were seeing. My husband looked at the girl giving us our order and said, "Man, did you see that?" The girl said, "Yes, I don't know what that was and I don't want to know what it was!" Richard and I decided to go home and watch the news

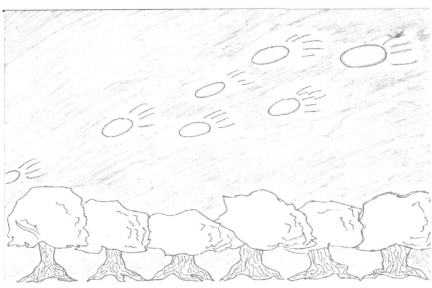

White objects flying over Raytown

to see if there were any other reports.

Sure enough, it was on the news that night that some people in eastern Kansas City had reported seeing some bright lights. The television station checked it out and said it was nothing to worry about as they found out it was just space junk burning up in the atmosphere.

Richard, being a pilot, has flown jets and small planes for many years. I feel very confident in his opinion of what we had seen. I started laughing at the news report and turned to Richard and asked him, "Do you think that was space junk burning up?" Richard said, "Hell no, not unless the space junk flies in a formation and comes in like it is making a landing!" I've since found that the news doesn't always tell it like it is and is a part of the UFO cover-up.

The really strange thing about this sighting is that where we saw these things landing was in the exact same area that my brother had seen the UFO thirteen years earlier while he was working for Wayne! This area was still pretty much unchanged with a lot of woods and pastures. There is plenty of room out there for UFO's to be landing and taking off.

My husband's father lived in Denver Colorado, so we took many trips to Colorado. One year Richard took me to Ouray in his Jeep to do some four- wheeling. We traveled over the Million Dollar Highway and spent a couple of nights at a motel that was nestled in a valley with mountains surrounding it. Richard loved adventure and the four-wheel trails were not far from the motel.

The first trail we took was called "Pucker Pass" and it was rightly named! There were spots that were so narrow that the Jeep wheels were just inches from falling off the path, which would have sent you down the side of the mountain. When we first got to the motel we unloaded our Jeep and

Pucker Pass   Photo: Jean Walker

began to settle into our room. I immediately had the strangest feeling in that motel room. There was a corner open closet area to the right of our beds that I kept feeling someone, or I should say something, was watching us from. Here was that old feeling of being watched again.

We decided to relax that first evening so we went to dinner then came back to the motel. Then we put on our swimsuits and went out to sit in the Jacuzzi. It was so pretty with the mountains surrounding us. We just sat in the Jacuzzi relaxing, talking, and enjoying the scenery and drinking our wine. When we got back to our room that terrible uneasy feeling hit me again. I can't explain how I felt except to say things did not feel normal, and I felt watched. I did not like how uneasy this room made me feel.

We got up the next morning, had breakfast, and headed out for Pucker Pass. All morning I still had that strange feeling and I told Richard about it. He was always very sympathetic to my feelings and said he would stay on alert too, for anything unusual.

We headed down the trail it was a warm, sunny day, perfect for an adventure of going four-wheeling. We reached a very narrow area with boulders that had rolled down the mountain and I was screaming, "Stop, stop! I am not going any further in this Jeep!" I was looking down the mountainside from my viewpoint and it didn't look as if there was any room for the Jeep to get through. It appeared that the vehicle's wheels were right on the edge of the road and the road was narrowing even more.

We both got out of the Jeep and were surveying the trail. We were walking around to see if we could make it past the narrowing of the road and the boulders. Again, I felt watched. I told Richard, "Something is wrong. I know we are being watched!" Richard knew about my past with aliens and he knew what I meant by being

watched. I always felt Richard believed me about all that had happened to me concerning aliens. He never acted doubtful of me, so perhaps he had some of his own experiences that made him believe me.

While we were walking around the trail checking it out we begin hearing an owl hooting. This happened several times and we looked all around but could never see any owl. There weren't

Pucker Pass Photo: Jean Walker

even any trees around us at that point, there were just rocks and big boulders around us. I remembered reading that owls were often associated with aliens. Sometimes you see or hear an owl, but it is not an owl- it is an alien disguising its self to look or sound like an owl. This is how aliens sometimes cloak themselves so humans don't know they are around. Then I looked at Richard and said, "Oh, crap that's an owl and I have been feeling watched!" It seemed so weird that here we were literally miles away from everyone and I was feeling watched and now we were hearing an owl!

I told Richard I wasn't getting in that Jeep and trying to go through that dangerous pass area and he just laughed at me and said, "Okay, I will drive the Jeep and you just walk." That was fine with me because I didn't really know he would make it through that narrow path. Well, he did, but just barely, as I stood there watching him and holding my breath. I was scared to death as we drove on down the path. We got out of the Jeep several times that day and I swear we kept hearing an owl hooting! How strange and frightening that was, but we finally made it down through Pucker Pass. At the end of the pass was a beautiful green river that was gorgeous. We were able to pick up the highway from there and head back to the motel.

Back at the motel, I had that terrible, almost overwhelming feeling of being watched. I felt like there was something standing in the corner of the room, but I couldn't see anything. We shut the television off and both us went to sleep, tired from our big adventure that day.

In the middle of the night, I woke up and could not move. I was totally paralyzed. I could only move my eyes, and I could see Richard fast asleep and facing towards the window in our room. I kept trying to move but could not move even a finger. I was looking out the window and could see lights that were red, white, and blue and were going around and around in a circle, rotating around. I kept thinking, *Richard, Richard, wake up*, but I couldn't talk or move and he never woke up. I laid there flat on my back unable to do anything, just watching those strange lights go around and around as they reflected in room. It was just terrifying! Then I just went back to sleep as if I had been knocked out.

The next morning, I woke up and everything seemed normal, I could talk, walk, move around, it was like the night had never happened! I got up and got dressed and told Richard, "We are leaving this place now!" I explained to Richard what had happened the night before and asked him if he remembered anything. He did not remember seeing

anything, not the lights or anything else. So we left the motel and that area of Colorado and finished our vacation. The rest of the vacation went normally, with no more strange happenings.

I recently found a book that goes into some of the mysteries of owls and aliens. I would strongly suggest reading it in order to understand some of the connections between owls and aliens. The name of the book is "The Messengers" written by Mike Clelland. He talks about owls, synchronicity and the UFO abductees, and the book has a foreword by Richard M. Dolan.

I have known of this connection for some time now and experienced a strange owl happening with one of my bigger UFO investigation cases. There were three other field investigators with me on this investigation. It was in the evening, and we were waiting for the sun to set to do some sky watching. In the meantime, we were walking around the witness's very large yard when we saw an owl land in one of the trees. It was a very large brown colored owl that turn out to be a Great Horned owl. I had my camera out taking pictures when this happened, and I started taking pictures of the owl in the tree.

I would take several shots, then slowly walk towards the tree that had the owl in it. Then I would take a couple of other photos and slowly walk closer to the owl. I was moving very slowly so as not to frighten the owl away. When I got within 25 feet of the owl it flew away. The owl was very large and it was amazing to watch it fly.

When I got home and downloaded the photographs into my computer only three pictures came out of the tree and there was no owl in them! What happened to all those pictures? The photo of the tree that had the owl in it was there, but in the photos there was no owl at all! Three investigators saw the owl with our naked eyes while taking pictures, yet it did not show up in the photos. We watched it for about 10 minutes or longer. How strange! There have been many UFO sightings by the witness and investigators at this location, so we felt this owl was most likely a screen memory for an alien.

Of course it is possible the UFO's really do contain aliens as many people believe, and the government is hushing it up. I wouldn't like to comment on that."

Stephen Hawking

Chapter 15

Strange Events in More Recent Years

Richard and I were married for six years and then divorced. We should have never separated for the reasons we did, but life happens. We are still the best of friends and I am grateful for that. I was single for fourteen years before I married my last husband Bill. Bill and I had been together for twelve years and married for four when he died of esophagus cancer. I couldn't believe that this could happen to me again- to lose another husband with cancer.

For years and years, I have been awakened from a sound sleep with someone calling my name. All I hear is "Jean" and I wake up. Most of the time I recognize the voice calling me. Often it is my mom or dad and sometimes my grandparents. A few times I have not recognized the voice, maybe I am in too deep of a sleep to recognize the voice. I think when this happens to me it is a relative letting me know they are still here with me. I am not frightened by it, but really don't like being woken up that way as it is a bit startling.

I also have felt someone sitting down on my bed, no one is ever there. Sometimes I just feel as if someone or something is nudging the bed and I wake up. It just gently moves my bed enough to wake me up. I have had this happened many times and I find nothing there when I wake up. After the last abduction, I now think when the aliens put me back in my bed it causes the bed to move enough that it wakes me up and I think someone is nudging the bed.

Margie tells me that sometimes it is my spiritual guide sitting on my bed or a loving relative just wanting to be close to me. I feel this is true, but I don't think that is the case all the time. I really feel that sometimes it is related to the alien abductions and that they manage to wake me up as they put me back in my bed.

May 2010- Face in Mirror

My brother, Ted, had just finished taking a hot shower and while he was drying off he looked into the bathroom mirror. He was shocked when he looked up at the mirror and he saw the face of Jesus. It looked like the face on the famous shroud of Turin and it stayed there a couple of minutes, apparently looking at him.

This reminded me about how my mother, twenty years earlier saw Jesus looking very sad on her lampshade. She woke up in the middle of the night. Mom said she had never seen such sad eyes and she knew what it meant.

Now, my brother saw Jesus' face in his mirror, and that was just two weeks after my husband Bill had been diagnosed with cancer. We didn't know at that point that it would be terminal for Bill. He was given six months to a year to live, but he lasted for three years before passing. Once again, do you think this was a coincidence? I don't. I think things happen for a reason. Jesus was preparing my mother and brother for a bad family situation ahead of them.

In 2010, I started writing down strange things that happened to me, which is why I am giving the dates now. I wish I had started doing this many years before, just keeping a journal of happenings in my life. So many things happened to me on almost a weekly basis that without writing it down, I could not remember all of it. Unfortunately, I get busy and sometime forget to write things down, so even now there are some gaps in the dates. Frankly, in writing this book, I know there are things I have failed to mention or remember. It only dawned on me to start writing occurrences down after I became an investigator for MUFON. Now I realize the importance of keeping a journal and have asked many of my witnesses to do the same. My brother has helped me out a lot with remembering things from the past and between the two of us, I feel I have captured most of it.

In the spring of 2010, I started waking up on a regular basis at 2:30 or 3:00 am. I would wake up feeling like there was something outside watching me. It was strange because I would wake up out of a sound sleep for no apparent reason. On April 8, 2010, I woke up with scratches all over my left leg and it looked like someone had grabbed me. On April 20, I woke up with strange large red spot on my upper right chest area. The red spot then turned to a blistered looking area that was about three-inch by four-inch patch. I have no idea where this came from but it was a red, blistered patch of skin. It looked like a burn of some kind.

At the first part of May, my little Bichon dog Pepe would constantly look up and stare at nothing while were in bed watching television. Pepe would go over to the edge of the bed and growl softly, as if he could see something on that side of the bed. I got up went over and looked and of course there was nothing there. He is the only animal in my house, so there was no cat under the bed or anything else that I could see. I found this to be an uneasy, creepy feeling to have the dog just staring at nothing and growling. I knew he was seeing or sensing something that I couldn't.

June 2010- Big Flies

I was doing dishes and started seeing all these huge black flies in the kitchen. I am very clean and if there is one thing I can't stand, it's having nasty flies in my kitchen! These weren't just normal house flies- they were huge. I have never had flies in the house like this unless we had had the doors open for some reason, and we had not. I got the fly swatter and started killing the nasty little creatures and the more I killed them, the more that seemed to appear! I looked all over trying to figure out where they were getting in, but could not figure it out. This went on for about two days and then they just disappeared as quickly as they had shown up. It reminded me of the movie "Amityville Horror" when the flies showed up.

September 2010- Mom's Plate After my mother passed I took some of her hanging plates, one of which now hangs in my dining room. It is a framed plate that is the picture of an old-fashioned quilt. Mom had numerous plates but this one

was always one of my favorites and it had a nice wooden frame.

One day I was sitting on my couch in the living room and looked up at the plate. My dining room and living room are all an open area where you can easily see from one room to another.

Suddenly I could see a man's face in the plate! This plate has been in my dining room for years, so how was it I never saw this man's face in this plate before? When I got up and walked in front of the plate I could not see the face any longer. However, if you back up about 10 to 12 feet from the plate, his face shows up in the plate. I took pictures of it but it is a bit tough seeing the man's face, maybe you can make it out by turning the book horizontally – his mouth and beard are where the flowers are in the center. But it sure freaks my friends out! There is also a gold cross on the plate which is easy to see when you look straight on at it. I wonder if the maker of this quilt plate knows about this and I wonder if there is any meaning to it.

October 2010- Blood Smears
I was coming up the basement steps when I noticed there was a large blood smear on the wall. The walls are painted white, and the blood smear was light but it was obvious what it was. I asked my husband if he had done it somehow, but he said, "No I have no idea how it got there." It was up high and just a very strange place to see such a thing. I took a picture of it and washed the blood off the wall.

November 2010- Flying What?
My husband, Bill, and I were driving home from having dinner at my brothers in Blue Springs. I looked up to the southern sky and saw something that looked very strange. It looked like eight planes flying in a close formation, but then it turned and it looked like it was just one very large craft. It had no lights visible although it was still light outside, so lights might not have shown up. It was very large, bigger than a jumbo jet, had no wings, and I think it was more of a triangle shape. I was driving so it was hard for me to see it

and drive at the same time.

I asked my husband what he thought it could be. He said he thought it could be a UFO. This was a strange thing for him to say because he always said he didn't believe in UFOs and I was shocked by his answer. The object just disappeared. I kept looking towards the south all the way home, but never saw it again. Through MUFON we have had many reports of UFO's and strange lights in the Blue Springs area, so I would just assume this was another one of them. We have also had a lot of triangle shaped crafts reported in this area and I do believe this object I was seeing could have been a triangle.

December 2010- Face on Wall

I was in my bedroom getting dressed one morning and this time I had my overhead light on. Normally I just use the lamps. I happened to look up at the wall and noticed a really scary face in the paint. I was shocked as I had painted this room myself and had never noticed this face on the wall. I took a picture that did come out very well but found it very upsetting, mostly because I had never noticed it before. I now have a huge picture hanging over it. Hopefully when I get around to repainting again it will disappear. Just another strange thing I noticed- but why do I see so many faces in everything?

November 2011- UFO Sighting

I woke up one morning out of a dead sleep at 5:00 am because I felt someone sit down on my bed. I quickly rolled over, looking to see who it was, but there was no one there! It was a frightening way to be woken up. My morning got stranger on my way to work that day. I was traveling south on Sterling street in Independence when I spotted a super bright light in the western sky. At first, I thought it might be a helicopter and the morning sun was reflecting off it making it look like a light. I watched this bright light as it was traveling towards the south for about 30 seconds. Then the light just disappeared. It just vanished!

After I had gone about three miles further the light appeared again, and it was still traveling the same direction to the south. About a minute later it just disappeared again. I never saw it again but I really think it was a UFO. There were no flashing lights on this object like a plane would have and it was just one ball of bright, white light. Planes don't just vanish out of sight either and then reappear going the same direction in the same track line. It was a beautiful day with blue skies and no clouds, so there was no way the object could have disappeared behind clouds.

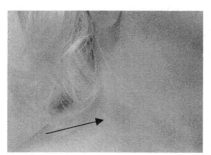

August 2011- Vampire Bites?
I woke up with two puncture wounds on the left side of my neck about four inches below my ear. They looked like I had been bitten by a vampire, and they hurt! The next day I didn't feel well and I had my husband look at my neck. The wounds were red and swollen. I had just gone to a MUFON conference two days before this happened. I told my husband that maybe the aliens had taken me and planted something in my neck. That night I got very sick, I woke up that morning covered in sweat and soaking wet. I did start to feel better by the next day. Another coincidence? I had just gone to a UFO conference and I woke up with this wound in my neck?

September 2011- Mom is Back

I had just had a bladder procedure done and had come home from the hospital. I went to bed and right to sleep after getting home. Then I felt someone rubbing my head. I knew it was my mother. She was comforting me and telling me everything was going to be okay. This dream was so real that I have a hard time believing it was just a dream. I really feel my mother was with me and giving me comfort after my procedure.

I often feel someone rubbing my head. It is more like they are just touching my hair in a soothing manner. This even happens to me when I am awake in bed watching television at night. I can tell that I am really being touched by someone and I think it is someone who really cares about me. Bill use to rub my head this way as if to comfort me or to let me know he loved me. This never frightens me when it happens because I know it is someone who cares about me. My husband, Bill, passed away May 20, 2013 from cancer. Therefore, I think after my procedure in 2011 it was my mother, but I do think Bill is patting me on my head now.

August 2013- Back Rub

I was sleeping at 2:00 a.m. and woke just enough to roll over on to my right side. Just as I rolled over I felt someone taking their hand and running it firmly right down my upper back. It scared the hell out of me! I quickly jerked my head back to the left to see who was there, but no one was there. This really freaked me out. I just laid there flat on my back afraid to turn to the other side. My little dog Pepe was at my right side, he was fast asleep and seemed not to notice of anything going on. I laid there for about an hour before I could go back to sleep. I knew for sure what I had felt. but who or what it was it? My personal feeling is that it was Bill because that just seemed like something he would do.

September 2013- Waking Phone Calls & Coffee

My cell phone rang at about 7:30 a.m. and I was fast asleep but got up to look at the phone. It appeared as an "unknown" number so I just went back to bed, but I couldn't sleep and I got up an hour later. I went into the kitchen to turn on my coffee pot (I always make it up the night before) and my coffee was already done!

Wow, this was very strange because you must flip the button to turn the coffee maker on, and then it takes several minutes to finish. I couldn't believe it! I just stood there and stared at the coffee pot thinking *what the hell?*

The coffee was fresh. It wasn't stale like it had been on for hours. Bill always loved having coffee with me in the mornings, and I really felt it was he who turned the coffee pot on. I think Bill woke me up with the phone call so I could drink my coffee fresh. He always said, "Nothing is as good as that first sip of fresh coffee in the morning." Later that morning I checked my phone again for that number that woke me up and there was no number - it just said "unknown".

October 2013- Finding Lost Items

I was looking in the bookcase next to the fireplace for a book that belonged to my great grandmother Nettie. The book was about psychics and I wanted to read all the things she had written in the margins. I found the book, and inside it I found an envelope with one of her cards and a matchbook cover with her information for spiritual readings. I read some of the book and her writings. That night I had a dream about her. She told me I had the psychic gift, too, and I just needed to trust in myself using my instincts. I was sick with a cold and there was some real confusion about some of the dream, but I felt I did get the drift of what she was trying to tell me.

I had been looking for a picture of her- the one where she won the beauty contest when she was 18 years old. I had gone through many pictures in search of that one and I knew I had it somewhere. I had been looking for it for several years. The next day after this dream, I went to the basement to look for some curtains I wanted to hang. The very first box I opened, I found Nettie's picture I had been looking for and I found it under the curtains! What a strange place to find it packed and how strange the timing was in finding it the day after I had had the dream of her talking to me. Another coincidence?

November 2014- Triangle UFO

It was a cold evening and I was driving home from the grocery store about 7:00 p.m. It was twilight, but still light enough to see things in the sky. As I crested a hill in Raytown, I saw strange lights flashing on something flying in the air. I could tell by the lights that it was not an airplane because there were just too many lights for a plane. After almost wrecking the car looking at the object I was able to pull off on to a side street that faced north where I could see the object from a good vantage point.

As I watched the object it turned sideways and I could see it was a triangle. It had a blue light in each corner of the triangle and in the center, was a large red light with smaller white lights around it. I was in such awe- seeing a triangle-shaped object, that I didn't think to get my camera out. I was afraid to take my eyes off it for fear it would disappear, and I really wanted to watch it as long as possible.

The object was coming from the north, then turned west

and continued at about the speed of a small prop plane. I watched it fly west until it was out of sight. The next day, I reported it to MUFON and worked the case myself. I looked everywhere on the internet and in the MUFON files, but could not find any other reports of anyone else seeing a triangle in this area of the state. I felt befuddled that no one else had seen it. However, since becoming a MUFON investigator, I find that this is not unusual and sometimes not everyone will see the same thing. For example, only three witnesses reported a very huge saucer shaped UFO hovering over the downtown area of Kansas City, Missouri at different times in 2011- 2012. The objects were very low over the buildings, yet no one else saw it or reported it. Something that huge over a large city should have been seen by many people. In one case, a woman was walking with three of her colleagues and saw a gigantic craft over the downtown buildings, yet her friends were oblivious to it. It seems that only some people can see these craft while others don't. I consulted Margie Kay about this and she said that she thinks some people have the ability to see things that vibrate at a higher rate, and this explains why not everyone sees some objects.

June 2014- More Dreams

I seem to have spells, or periods of time, when I have psychic dreams. In June 2014, I had a dream about my ex-husband Richard. In my dream, we were together again. I was so happy! It was as if I was living in a wonderland and everything was just wonderful in my life. Maybe I fell in the rabbit hole, I can't explain it! It was like a happily-ever-after fairy tale.

The dream was so vivid that after I had my coffee I sent an email to Richard letting him know about my dream and how happy I woke up right afterwards. Richard now lives in Colorado and is remarried. Later that day he wrote to me saying; Wow, I can't believe this, but at the same time you were having that dream (about 8:00 a.m. my time) his present wife was taking a walk with her neighbor. A good size rock fell off the cliff hitting his wife on the head. It was such a bad accident that the neighbor lady took her right to the hospital. Months later she is still having speech problems from her brain swelling and she was off work for three months.

That same weekend this happened Richard found out that his first wife and mother of his two children had terminal brain cancer. She has since passed.

I cannot control what I dream, but I really do feel terrible about what happened to his other wives. I don't know if these events related to my dream, but here again, we are talking about coincidences.

September 2014- A Premonition Dream

I sat straight up in bed out of a dream about 8:00 a.m. thinking "That no good, lousy woman my father married, is now buried next to my father"! I was irate with anger. When my dad divorced my mother, then married this other woman, I blamed her for breaking up my parent's marriage. I never cared for my new stepmother, and only tolerated her for my dad's sake. But out of the blue here I was, dreaming about her burial, but I didn't know if she was dead or alive.

My dad once told my brother that he regretted divorcing my mother and marrying this other woman. He said she was a real witch and that she made his life miserable. When my dad was killed, this woman never gave my brother or me a thing that belonged to my dad. She gave all of my dad's gun collection to her sons. I can't tell you how many times my dad told us in front of this woman that he wanted my brother to get his gun collection.

Because my dad had no will my brother and I got nothing. I despised the ground this greedy witch walked on. So I sat up in bed that morning and said out loud, "That witch is buried next to my father!" Why would she want to do that? All she ever did was talk bad about my dad to anyone who would listen to her. I know because a lot of it got back to me. I guess because my dad had already paid for the cemetery plots she used it, but I know it wasn't because she cared about him or him for her, for that matter.

A few days later my son and I were heading downtown and had to go right past the cemetery where my dad is buried. I looked at Tom and said, "I am going to stop by Papa Ted's grave," and then I told him about my dream. Tommy just looked at me as if he didn't know what to think, but we stopped by grave site. I knew my step-mother had been in a nursing home for years but knew nothing else about her. Sure enough she had died August 19, 2014 and the day we visited the site was October 31, 2014. Her grave was fresh and the grass hadn't even started to grow on it yet.

I was just furious that she was buried there next my dad, and Tommy was shocked at what I had told him and for us to find out it was true. I asked him, "Would you have believed me about my dream if I hadn't told you about it before we stopped here?" He said, "Well mom, I don't know if I really would have or not. Wow, I can't believe how you pick up on things, it's scary sometimes."

Why did I have this dream? My dad had been gone for 30 years. I think I picked up on my father's thoughts or spirit, just like I kept having that repetitive dream of something of his being in my grandmother's closet. I think my dad really despised this woman for the misery she caused him and for what she had done to our family. I don't think he wanted her buried next to him and I picked up on it. I think Dad was trying to tell me that in the dream because what else could explain it? What other reason he would he want me know about it? Just another coincidence- her dying and I sensed it within a two-month period.

August 2015- Ghost?

Again, while I was lying in bed watching television as my little dog Pepe slept next to me. Pepe woke up and rose to slowly creep over to the edge of the bed with the hair on his back standing up and softly growling. When he finally reached the edge of the bed, he looked down and then jumped back toward me as if he was afraid of whatever it was he saw. I got up and walked around the bed but could see nothing there. Pepe got up right against me when I got back in bed, it was as if he was still afraid. He was afraid of whatever he had seen on the other side of the bed. Sometimes I catch him just staring at the wall on that side of the bed, but there is never anything there that I can see. It creeps me out when he does this. It is a known fact that animals can sense and see things that humans cannot, and Pepe saw something that was scaring him for some time.

"The longer one lives, the more mysterious life seems."

Francis Brett Young

Chapter 16

MUFON, Extraterrestrials, and Cryptic Animals

I joined MUFON in 2011. I decided I wanted to become an investigator for the Mutual UFO Network order to get more information about extraterrestrials and UFOs and help solve the mystery. The first thing you must do is to purchase the MUFON manual, study it, take the Field Investigator test, then go out in the field on investigations with experienced investigators. I went through all the steps for MUFON and became a field investigator in 2011. As of August of 2015, I became a Star Team Investigator and Section Director of the Kansas City Chapter of MUFON.

Margie Kay is the Assistant State Director of Missouri MUFON and lives here in Kansas City. Debbie Ziegelmeyer is the State Director of Missouri MUFON and lives in St. Louis. Debbie is also a board member at MUFON. Both these ladies have been a huge help in teaching me the ropes about being a good investigator, and like most jobs, it's an ongoing process.

One of the first MUFON cases I worked was with a couple here in Raytown where I live. They lived about a mile from me as the crow flies. When I was questioning the witness, he told me he saw a UFO while standing in the parking lot of his apartment complex.

He told me when he first saw the UFO, it was to his northeast and he felt it was not far away from him – perhaps a mile away. That would have put it right over my house! Then he told me about what had happened the day after he reported his sighting to MUFON. He was watching TV in his living room while he sitting next the windows. He happened to look outside the window and he saw two new, black pickup trucks go past his apartment.

He said they were following each other very closely and then they slowed down to almost a dead stop right in front of his place. He said the windows were darkened in the trucks and but he felt like they were staring at him from the vehicles. Then the trucks slowly drove off and he never saw them again. I think this sounds like the men in black (MIBs).

About a week later I was on my computer working on some MUFON cases. My office is in a spare bedroom with three very large windows. Two windows face the street, which is a main street, and the other window faces my patio and back yard. I saw someone out of the corner of my eye go past the two windows facing the street. Since my yard is fenced in for my dog, and all the gates have padlocks on them this was very concerning.

At first, I thought maybe my son, who was still living here at the time, had gone out to the patio, but when I looked out of the window nobody was out there. I got up from the computer and went outside. I saw no one in any part of the yard. If anyone had been in my yard, they would have had to jump the fence to get out. I came in and went downstairs to the basement where my son was and asked him if he had been outside and quickly came back in the house. He said, "No Mom, I have been down here the whole time." Who did I see walk quickly past my windows? And how did they get out of the large yard so quickly? And this all happened while I was working on my MUFON cases. Was this yet another coincidence!

A Big Case

I received a very active case in Eastern Independence, Missouri to investigate. There has been so much activity with this case, which is still ongoing, that it could be the subject of my next book. I have been working on this case for about 18 months now and things just keep happening, and I am still looking for answers. I have four other investigators who have helped me work this case.

The witness reported to that she counted 32 lights which she thinks are unidentified objects. She stated they were flying right at each other on some occasions, and at times almost crashing into each other. I thought it sounded more like our military playing war games than UFOs. I happen to know through a good source that the military does war games in a location within 10 miles of where this case is located. I contacted Whiteman Air Force Base (WAFB) in Warrensburg, Missouri, and told them that I was trying to get some information. I asked them if they were conducting war games on this date and time in this area. I explain why I was inquiring and that I was a field investigator for MUFON, and had this strange report from at witness that I was working on.

The Air Force wanted to know my name, address, phone number, and email address, which I gave them. Here is the email I received from them the following day:

Response to query

From: PFIESTER, JOEL R A1C USAF AFGSC 509 BW/PA (joel.pfiester@us.af.mil)
Sent: Wed 8/27/14 1:28 PM
To: jmwblondie@hotmail.com (jmwblondie@hotmail.com)
Cc: COOPER, JOHN M Capt USAF AFGSC 509 BW/PA (john.cooper.21@us.af.mil)

Jean,

Thanks for your query. For this and any future queries regarding this issue, as a matter of operational security, we will not discuss flight schedules and flight paths.

Very respectfully,

A1C Joel Pfiester
509th Bomb Wing Public Affairs
Photojournalist
509th BW/PA
DSN: 975-5727
Comm: 660-687-5727

I didn't think they would give me any useful information on what was happening that night. However, it was worth a try to see if I could acquire anything that might help, but no luck. I have nothing to hide, so I truthfully gave them all my reasons and all my personal information.

About two weeks later I got a new laptop and my friend Doug was helping set it up. We were working on connecting it to my Wi-Fi. When setting this up and are searching for Wi-Fi, it will show all the Wi-Fi connections that are close to you. Doug looked at me in shock and said, "What is the FBI Terrorist Attack Force doing in your neighborhood? Why would they be watching you? They have to be very close to you for this to show up the computer." He really felt they must have been very close by and most likely were monitoring me. I thought about it for a second and then said,

"Oh, I bet they are watching me because I called WAFB to see if they were conducting war games in this one area of Independence, Missouri where my case is located."

I immediately called Margie Kay and told her what had happened. She just laughed and said, "Okay, so now you have joined the ranks with the rest of us and they are on to you working on MUFON cases." In talking with other MUFON investigators, it seems almost all of them are being watched by the government. Honestly, I think they have been watching me for some time now, which would explain why I am seeing the helicopters over my house, someone unknown walking past my window while I was working on my MUFON cases, and all the computer problems I have encountered since I have become an investigator.

Several hours later we checked the Wi-Fi and the FBI was still there. I rarely ever check it now to see if they are still watching me as I really don't care. I am a law-abiding person and have nothing to hide from the FBI or anyone else. I can't help but feel they just want to find out how much I might know about what is going on with UFOs and any government connection. I am sure there are many government experiments going on that the military does not want the public to know about, and sometimes investigators get too close to the truth.

On the other hand, maybe they (the government) don't want the investigators to expose the real truth-- that there are aliens here and they have been here for a long time. Aliens are among us, they kidnap us, they do experiments on us and people disappear all the time and we never find them. The public is seeing more now in our skies and the digital cameras are picking up things that we can't see with the naked eye. I am astounded by some of the photos I have seen and I know for sure they are not photo-shopped.

We are being watched constantly by aliens. Not just one kind of alien, but many different types. I have photos that show alien craft in the air at all times of the day and night. These craft can morph and have cloaking devices that enable them to disappear from our sight, but they are still there, we just can't always see them.

Since the digital cameras can see more of the light spectrum than our eyes can, the cameras are picking up stuff that we just haven't seen before. Sometimes we can just see what looks like a disturbance in air (like waves) and we can tell it is a craft that is cloaking itself from our sight. Sometimes we can see outlines of these waves in pictures that look like the creature cloaking in the movie "The Predator."

In one of my cases, the witness has been able to slow the film down to where you can see the triangular crafts going into lakes or coming out of lakes. Many areas that we investigate, we find the UFOs are near or in water. Some UFOs have been known to hide in rivers, lakes, and the ocean; we think that perhaps in the larger bodies of water, they have UFO bases submerged in them.

I honestly think the UFOs hide in all types of water. I have the one case that the witness has numerous pictures of UFOs going into or coming out of some the lakes in my area. I have another case where the witness has seen UFOs coming out of the Missouri River. One time this witness saw the UFO hovering above the river with a stream of water being sucked up from the river into the craft. One theory is that perhaps the UFO is getting hydrogen out the water for fuel purposes, but we don't know for sure why this is happening.

Often people (witnesses) seeing these UFOs and the field investigators are being followed by government agencies. Sometimes they are not just being followed, but some have been taken. Kidnapped by the government. They have been told <u>not</u> to repeat the things they have seen or the experiences they have had or something bad will happen to them!

I know several people that have exposed too much information and have had terrible tragedies in their lives. When you have a tragic event in your life it can totally distract you from what you are working on. Other things can become more important to you than exposing an alien or government secret. I have seen this happen numerous times to people who are working on such matters. One person I knew who was involved in a deep UFO case died of a very fast growing rare cancer. We (investigators) think the reason was because they knew way too much about a prominent case or knew too much and were talking about their experience to others.

I am not going to say a lot more about this matter right now as I don't want to be one these people! Maybe it is already too late for me and I already know too much, I don't know, but I do not need to push my luck. I have two ongoing cases that I am working now and both are deep in conspiracy, again this would be another book in itself. This is not happening only in relation to my cases, but I have knowledge of several other investigators who have the same issues.

All I will say for now is there is just so much going on that the general public does not know about that it would blow everyone's minds! My suggestion is to get involved, join MUFON and attend MUFON meetings in your area. You will be amazed at what you may find out! Do your own research on the web and read everything you can find on the subject of UFOs.

December 2014- Fighter Helicopters

I heard numerous helicopters going very low over my house and it was very loud. So I went outside and going right over my house, moving from the southeast and heading northwest were five military fighter helicopters. Then about 30 minutes later they came back over the house heading east.

My friend, Claudia, came over for an early dinner with me that day. About 2 hours after she got here, we were talking at the kitchen table when the five helicopters went over my house again. They were not flying high, but just over the treetops, and they were heading north again.

A few minutes later my mailman knocked on the door to give me a package. I ask him if he had seen all those helicopters flying around the neighborhood. He said yes, they went over three times and they were very low. He told me that these types of helicopters are the ones that carry rockets on each side of the choppers. He said however, they did not have any missiles on them today, but he too wondered what they were up to. He said maybe we will see something on the news that night because there must be something going on. I watched the news on a couple of channels that evening and there was no mention of the helicopters.

In the two on-going cases that I am working right now both of the witnesses tell me that they have had fighter helicopters going over their houses. They think they are being watched. However, maybe the helicopters are looking for the UFOs that these witnesses are seeing. After finding out that the FBI was watching me, I couldn't help but wonder if they were not watching my witnesses too.

I am a science teacher and I feel we are constantly learning about new things going on in the world around us. One of the most important things you can do is always keep an open mind when something new is presented. There are many good UFO conferences around the U.S. and elsewhere. They provide a lot of good information and experienced speakers on the many different aspects of ufology. I personally find these conferences extremely informative and interesting. Then there are books- many books on the subject of UFOs.

I have also been involved with some ghost hunts and in dealing with the paranormal. I do find this subject interesting, as well as the UFO phenomena. For now though, I really enjoy my UFO investigations more than anything. This is most likely because of my past experiences of abduction and wanting to find some truth on the subject. However, I found in doing these investigations that the paranormal and cryptic animals often overlap with UFO experiences. It seems to all be related.

One of my cases in Independence was within a couple of blocks of the Community of Christ Temple (formerly Latter Day Saints), which is constructed in an odd manner as a spiral. This man had been taking pictures in the early morning hours (daylight) of lights that would morph. They would change shapes within just a few frames of shooting them. He ended his report with the statement, "I live next to the weird church in Independence."

One of the strangest things this man said to me was that he had been talking with a neighbor who lived just down the street. The two men were exchanging stories about seeing these morphing lights (craft), when his neighbor told him he had seen strange creatures coming up from the storm drains.

These storm drain openings are very close to the church. He said it was always at night when he would see these creatures. He was unable to see the creatures clearly, but they just looked more like creatures (not humans), but they were humanoid in shape. This seemed very strange.

All of this was happening just very close to the spiral-shaped temple. What I am going to tell you about now is just a rumor that I have heard and I have no evidence that it is true. So why am I am I talking about it? Because of all the UFO cases in the area surrounding the Temple and sightings of cryptid creatures and extraterrestrials.

The rumor is that the spiral church was built with a large antenna in it that spirals from below ground way up towards the sky as a communication device. This is a beautiful building, but it is strangely built with this spiral. Could that be the real reason for the spiral? I also have heard that the bottom basement level of this building is where the church elders and the aliens work together. Strange, but as we all know, sometimes rumors do have some truth to them and this could explain why the Independence area has so much UFO activity.

After hearing this rumor, I began to wonder if those storm drains don't have tunnels leading to the basement of this church. This could also explain why that man was seeing these creatures coming out of the storm drains at night. This could also explain the cryptic animal reports we keep receiving in this area. A small group of investigators want to check out these rumors of ET's and cryptic animals coming from the storm drains. We have a good idea of how we might conduct this investigation as we have discussed our plans and our best way to approach it. I will cover our findings in a future publication.

Community of Christ Temple in Independence, Missouri
Source: Wickimedia Commons

Possible Bigfoot Encounter

Then there's another cryptid animal - Bigfoot. One evening when I was working the on-going investigation in Eastern Independence, I had a very strange thing happen. This area is within a mile from the Missouri river, surrounded by farmland, caves, and power plants, with lots of forest and conservation land which it is full of many wild animals. One evening I was outside with the witness and her husband while we were sky watching. We started hearing a very strange loud yelling from an animal, and every time this terrible sound was made the coyotes would start howling along with all the dogs in the area. It was strange and frightening to hear this sound. It sounded like an animal in distress in some way. It was unlike any yelling I had ever heard. It would stop for a while, then in a few minutes it would do it again. I would say maybe five minutes or less apart. Again, when this thing would yell, the coyotes and dogs would start howling. I was raised in the country and I have never heard such a sound in my life. This happened about five times within a 30-minute time period. I had to leave soon after that, but would have liked to have stayed around for a while. My witness said they didn't hear it again, so I guess it stopped anyway.

After hearing this for myself, I looked at different Bigfoot websites to see if I could hear the same sound again. After several months of listening to these Bigfoot recordings, I finally found the one that fit what I had heard. They said on this clip that this sound was most like a screech owl, only when I heard it you knew from the volume and deepness of the yell it was not an owl! The yell was powerful, deep and chilling! You could hear the chesty deepness of this beast and you could tell it was very powerful.

I asked the couple if they knew what the sound was and they said no they hadn't heard it before. This yelling probably happened five times before I had to leave that night. Well, you know what I was thinking - Maybe it was a Bigfoot. This area could definitely support a Bigfoot and I have seen so many odd things happening in this area that it is a possibility.

It is a known fact that Bigfoot sightings and UFO sightings are often found in the same area at the same time. Often, we hear about strange lights being seen, then a Bigfoot is reported in the same general area. I have made sure I have a tape recorder with me every time I go to investigate this area since then. If I can get a recording, then I can have an expert in the study of Bigfoot listen to it. My witness in this case reported to me that she has heard this yelling two more times since the night I was out there in the last year.

Another strange coincidence concerning Bigfoot occurred in an area nearby before this case. A friend told me that her son-in-law, who is a die-hard skeptic, was with two of his friends and they were fishing near the Sugar Creek Conservation Area. There are a lot of woods in this area and two ponds where they were fishing. This is only about one mile from the location of the case where I heard this strange yelling take place that night on my investigation, and it is also near the Missouri River where there are a lot of woods. Three men were standing on the banks fishing when out of the woods walked a Bigfoot. The Bigfoot walked along the stream, looked in the water for something, then turned and walked back into the woods. The witness said that the creature was huge, about eight to nine feet tall and had reddish brown hair. He said he thinks the creature never even saw the three men fishing as they were just quietly standing there and had not been talking for some time. He said all three of them looked at each other, then without saying a word, they picked up their stuff, then quietly and quickly ran for their cars. Could this have been the same creature that I heard yelling just a couple of months later?

More Criptids

Lately, there have been numerous reports of very large wolf-like creatures in the area that we suspect to be cryptid animals. These reports are hard to prove or disprove but some of the reports have been made by some very reliable people. We have also had some reports of a very strange kangaroo type animal with extremely long ears. Not a real kangaroo, but a cryptic animal that looks a lot like a kangaroo for a lack of being able to describe it any other way. This has been reported to investigators by several different reliable people in different areas surrounding Kansas City and the outlying areas.

I had another report in the same area of Independence (same area as the Bigfoot) of a rather strange looking creature that had a resemblance of a kangaroo. This creature was just sitting in the middle of a country road and wouldn't move. This lady was with her husband and they had just left a park by the Missouri River. They had to drive around this creature as it just sat there looking at them. She said her husband looked at her and said, "What in the hell is that thing?" With all these reports, it surely makes me wonder what is going on with all these cryptic type animals being seen by so many different people.

The city dump, Missouri River, and the Conservation Area are right in the heart of the area in Independence that so many of these reports are being made. I found two creeks that run out of the dump and through the woods. These creeks dump into the Missouri River after winding through the wooded area where I am sure many animals drink from. I am going to take some water samples and get them tested to see what shows up in the creek water. There is so much pollution in these large dumps (chemicals), who knows what these animals could be drinking? I wonder if the creeks could be polluted enough to cause mutations in the animals.

March 2015- Abducted Again?

Margie Kay asked me to join her on a trip to Springfield, Missouri where she was doing a presentation for a paranormal convention. I helped Margie at her table selling her books, and we spent two nights there. The second night we were there I woke up in the middle of the night and I caught a glimpse of something gray going around the corner at the foot of my bed. It looked kind of strange to me but I figured it had to be Margie Kay going to the bathroom. Who else would be going that way, right? I tried to look over to the other bed to see if Margie was in her bed but I couldn't move. I was paralyzed. The figure looked gray in color and had a humanoid shape to it, but that was all that I could see. Then I just fell back to sleep as if nothing had happened. None of this seemed right to me, so the next morning I asked Margie, "Did you get up and use the bathroom last night?" She said, "No, I was so tired last night I don't think I woke up at all." So I told Margie about what I had seen and we both knew something very strange had happened, we just couldn't remember what it might have been.

We left the motel that morning and Margie wanted to do some work on a case of hers. We went to the witness's house to pick up a video where he said he had taped an alien that was in his back yard. We watched the video at the witness's house and it sure appeared to be a grey alien peeking from behind a tree and going back and forth several times and for at least 15 minutes. We left with the Sony video tape in hand to head for home. Margie said, "Now keep an eye out on the way home and make sure no one is following us."

We made it home with no unusual events happening. However, when Margie reviewed the video tape on her computer the alien we saw was completely gone. The video of the tree and back yard was there, but there was no alien in the video. We thought that was extremely strange. Someone had to have removed the alien from the video because we know what we saw.

That evening I was watching TV at home and my nose started to bleed. It wasn't bad, but it is very unusual for me to have a nosebleed. The next morning, I was getting dressed and I noticed I had a red rash on my left chest area right below my shoulder. It covered an area about three by four inches so I decided to take a picture of it. I have recently decided taking pictures of such things is a good way to keep evidence. I wish I had thought of that many years ago. The rash was gone after about three days and it did not itch. My nose was so sore on the second day that I couldn't touch it as it was so painful. It took several more days for my nose to heal.

A few days later, I was talking with Margie about the rash I had on my chest and asked her if she had experienced anything since we had gotten home. She told she had not had anything physical show up on her, but she now did remember something about the night I saw the Grey walking towards the bathroom. She said, "I remember seeing something come in the door of the motel and I think maybe we were both abducted, which would explain why I was so exhausted the next day."

So I guess Margie saw them come in and I saw them leaving! Perhaps someone came into the room, took the tape, and erased the alien from it, then returned the tape to the bag it was in. There is really no other explanation. Whoever did this must have had a good reason to cover it up.

Experiencers Group

I started going with to an Experiencers Group where people that feel they are being abducted can talk about it with other experiencers. I have found these meetings to be very helpful and it is good place to be able to talk about your own experiences with the comfort of being free from any ridicule. I also find that I am remembering more and more about my abductions and I have had some real emotional moments in this group. The leader of our group tells me that I will continue to remember more as we go along with our meetings.

I am going to have some regression done to see if that will allow me to remember some the things that have happened to me. I would really like to remember a lot more details. Right now it is like a puzzle. I have a lot of the pieces and I am trying to put it all together, but some pieces are still missing. Maybe my mind just can't handle all of the truth at once, but I am working on it and I am remembering more all the time. I hope that being hypnotized will help me remember much more of what has happened and maybe someday I can complete the puzzle.

In April 2015- Abducted?

I keep waking up with bruises and scratches and have no idea how they occurred. I noticed today that there were three bruises about the size of nickel, one under each arm close to my armpit area and one on the center of my pelvis bone. I was really concerned, and wondered - how does a person get a bruise under each underarm (triceps area) and in the same spot on both arms? I couldn't figure it out, so I showed them to my some of my investigator friends and they immediately all said the same thing, "It looks like someone or something was carrying you - one on each arm and their fingers left bruises." Well, you can't bump your underarms hard enough to get bruises and this made sense of how I could have gotten them in the triceps area. I still don't know how I got the bruise on my pelvis and maybe it is better I don't know.

I also showed my friend Claudia the bruises because I share most things with her. She sat and thought about it for a moment and then said, "It looks like someone was carrying you and kind of forcibly." So did I get abducted again? I think it sure fits the pattern. I just wish I had more answers.

June 12, 2015- Another Implant?

I woke up with my nose being very sore again. It is the same as last time- the left side of my nostril, and it is so sore I can't touch it. My nose remained sore until the 20th of June when I had another small nosebleed. This time I felt as if my nose was in the healing stage for the first time since March when all this started. I think whatever it was in my nose had worked its way out. My nose started to feel much better after this happened.

Now I wondered, did an implant dissolve or fall out? Are they going to abduct me again to put in another implant? The fear starts to increase again as I wonder about all of these happenings. I also started wondering if the implant was something that was monitoring my health in some way or was a tracking device? My sciatic nerve in my left hip has been killing me for about three weeks now - is there a connection to the implant? I have even wondered if the aliens are trying to heal me sometimes, instead of doing damage to me. I'm fearful because I really don't know what is going on most of the time.

June 22, 2015- Hearing Voices

I was driving home and was close to my house. It was about 10:00 am, and I was on a quiet side street when I heard a woman's voice. It sounded like it was in the car with me, right next to me. I had the windows up as it was a hot day, so the AC was on and there was nobody around. I could hear her voice but was having great difficulty understanding what she was saying. I was mostly startled to hear a voice in the car with me. I think what I heard her say was something about a cause, and there was a natural way or nature's way to deal with it. I immediately thought of the terrible sciatic nerve pain in my hip that had been killing me for some time now and wondered if it had something to do with that. This nerve pain had become so bad, it was disabling at times, in that I couldn't do some things I really wanted to do because of the pain and I was becoming very concerned over it.

I had heard the voice so clearly that I grabbed my phone to see if that could have been the voice but my phone showed nothing, no one's name was on it. I checked the radio and it was off as I rarely listen to it in the car anymore. This was a very strange thing to have happen, and it had never happened to me before.

June 23, 2015- Strange Calls and Premonitions

I was in the kitchen at the sink and had just gotten off the computer in the office when my house phone rang. I had the TV on in the dining room and when my phone rings it always shows the number calling on the TV. I looked up at the TV and it said "Ms. Jean Walker," and it had my home number as the caller, which was the number it was calling in on!

I had not even been on my home phone that morning. I just stood there in amazement looking at my name and number on the TV wondering how could this happen. I decided to answer it just to see what would happen, but when I did it was just dead sound with no dial tone and no one talking. This was weird and kind of frightening.

I talked with Margie a few days later and told her what had happened to me. She remote-viewed it and told me that my spiritual guides and ET's were trying to communicate with me and that I needed to meditate daily and I would get to where I could hear them. I have a gut feeling Margie is right and that was probably an ET guide who was trying to help me heal my hip pain.

I am also developed a gut feeling I shouldn't go to St. Louis the next week to hear a speaker at the St. Louis MUFON Chapter. I had made plans with another investigator to go to hear this speaker on Bigfoot and I really wanted to hear them, but something kept telling me not to go at this time. I listened to my gut this time and canceled my trip.

My feeling that I should not going to St. Louis was right on! My friend Claudia was going to stay at my house with Pepe while I was gone. The morning I would have been going to St. Louis, Claudia fell in her kitchen with a crock pot in her hands that broke into pieces cutting her finger and her arm. She had to have seven stitches in her arm and she was fairly beat up, she was also very sore for several days. No way could she have made it to care for Pepe and I would not leave my dog alone because of his health issues.

On the same day the trip would have been on we had three tornado warnings put out and one of the tornadoes touched down briefly just four blocks from me. It was as if the sky had opened up as we had about three inches of rain in a 24-hour period. Well my finished basement flooded. Luckily, my friend Doug came over and helped me out that day and we were able get the flooding under control without much damage to the basement.

I'm glad I stayed home to deal with Pepe and the flooding. Claudia would not have been able to do all of this for me since she was injured and couldn't have done it. My instincts were right on, and yes, I think my guides were telling me clearly not to leave. I say always listen to your gut instincts because there is a reason you have them, and I have never regretted listening to mine.

June 30, 2015- ET's or spirits wanting my attention?

When I woke up that morning I opened my bedroom door and I heard the doorbell ringing and ringing. As soon as it stopped ringing it would start again, like someone kept pushing the button over and over again. I always look out before I answer my door, so I peeked out the window where I can see the door and there was no one there. It is a wireless doorbell so I unplugged the ringer from the wall socket to stop it, and then just out of curiosity I opened the door and looked around, but saw nobody in the area.

Later that morning as I left the house to get into my car, I pressed the keypad to unlock the door, only it didn't work, and the door would not unlock. I finally had to use the key to get into my car and strangely, even though when I used the key, my car alarm went off.

I went to the store and when I came out the locks worked fine with the automatic key opener. I went home, unloaded the groceries, and again the automatic key opener was working fine and it has worked ever since. My car is parked just outside my house, a few feet from the door that had the doorbell problem that morning. I don't know what that has to do with anything, except they are in the same proximity and it all happened on the same morning. Two days later I plugged the doorbell chime back in and it has worked fine ever since.

I feel like there was something trying to get my attention since it was such a strange thing to happen. My back pain had also started to really improve with some deep massage therapy and general therapy, which was just as the voice told me- to use a natural way to help heal. I feel something or someone was trying to get my attention and get me listen to them. Sometimes though, I think my life is so strange!

July 10, 2015- Was I fighting an Abduction?

As I was putting on my makeup this morning I was looking in the mirror and noticed I had a deep scratch on the left outer part of my wrist. It was about two and half inches long. Then I saw another scratch right above my left elbow. I couldn't believe I woke up with these scratches, and kept asking myself how this could have happened without realizing it. My nails are well manicured, so that couldn't have been the cause. I would think I would have awakened when this happened because the scratches were so deep and red.

I showed four other investigators these scratches and they determined that I must have been fighting whoever was trying to take me because these scratches looked like defense wounds. We also decided that since I enter my bed on the left side (which would be the side where someone would grab me) that it would make sense that these wounds were on my left arm. Now that is scary, but made good sense that this could be one scenario as to how I received these wounds.

That night I was pulling a shoe out from under my bed and a pill bottle rolled out. Then I remembered that I had the pill bottle sitting on the bookcase next to bed the night before so I would remember to refill it. The bookcase is located right across from my bed about two feet away on the opposite wall of the bed. I thought OMG, I bet I was fighting with something and that is how the pill bottle got knocked off and rolled under my bed. There is no other way I can explain all of this, so I think they took me again. That would explain the pill bottle and the type of scratches I had received.

I am beginning to think that "they" want to tell me something, it's just a feeling I have after hearing that voice 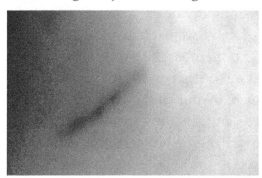 and so many things happening to get my attention. I wish I could remember what happened to me and what they do or tell me. I think regression is in my future. The photo only shows the deeper wound but I can't get the other photo to print off for this book. There were three deep scratches on the side of my left arm.

August 2015- Knocking Again?

I was mopping the kitchen floor and I heard someone knocking on my door. I looked out the kitchen window, but saw no car in the driveway but didn't look out to see if anyone was at the door knocking. I was busy so I just went back to mopping and then I hear the doorbell ring. This time I looked out the front bedroom window where I can see the door and no one was there! I then opened the door and looked around but there was no one in sight. Again, I wonder why is there knocking and doorbell ringing when no one is there? What is going on?

An investigator friend tells me that he has heard that many times before - when ET's abduct someone they will knock at the door. Is this what is going on around here?

September 2015- They are coming for me next

I had a nightmare and it scared me so badly that I woke up in A-Fib, but I could not remember the dream. I think I was more concerned about waking up with A-fib, but I knew why it had happened- because of the dream.

A week later, I woke up feeling my heart racing again as if I was going into another A-Fib. I had just had another nightmare, only this time I remember the dream. In it someone had told me that terrorists were in my neighborhood and they were taking all the young men out of the houses into the yards and shooting them in the head. Then I was standing in my kitchen when terrorists dressed in black face hoods stormed in through my front door. They grabbed a young man (maybe it was my son) but in the dream I did not recognize him. The men were carrying the man forcefully out of my house to the front yard where he looked at me with terror in his face and said, "You are next. They will kill you next." They then shot and killed the young man and were headed back in the house for me.

I don't think this is exactly how these things happen, but perhaps the dream is telling me this could come about in our country and we need to be prepared. Maybe even though I saw this happening, it was really in another country and I was feeling what it would be like to live there, such as in the middle east. The terror was real though, and I hope it's not something that is going to happen in the USA.

This dream seemed important to me because I have never had a dream that scared me so badly I woke up in A-Fib. I am not making a predication though, just telling what my dream was about. Another thought that occurred to me is that perhaps it was not terrorists but it could have been extraterrestrials taking someone and I knew they were coming back for me next. And maybe that was my son the ET's took first.

September 24, 2015- Unwanted Visitors

I was sitting at my kitchen table looking into my living room. I started to see these strange wiggly lines or waves coming up from the floor to the height of about four feet. It looked a lot like heat waves you see on the hot pavement in the summertime. It lasted for several minutes then dissipated. I felt like something was there and it was trying to cloak itself so I wouldn't see it.

Later, I was running the sweeper in the front hallway by the door. I started smelling this terrible odor of something dead. It smelled like rotting, decaying flesh, which is a very distinctive smell that you don't mistake for anything else. I couldn't determine where the smell was coming from. However, the attic opening is in this hallway and I thought perhaps a squirrel died in the attic. Maybe I was smelling something dead in the attic and it was rotting. I went ahead and ran the sweeper through my house and then I went back to the hallway and there was no bad smell at all - it was completely gone.

A really odd thing about this smell was that a week earlier I was running the sweeper in the basement and I smelled the same thing. That time I thought maybe a mouse had died in the drop ceiling but again, I went back to the same spot a couple of hours later and there was no bad smell. Maybe I should stop running the sweeper as things are always happening to me when I do!

On the same day, I was getting dressed to go to a very early poker party with my class reunion friends and Claudia was going with me. It was around 1:30 p.m. and I had just finished doing my makeup and hair in the bathroom. I was dressed except for putting on my blouse and I walked into my bedroom. All of a sudden I started hearing a very loud pounding on the side of my house. I kind of stood there in shock thinking who and why would someone be pounding like that on the side of my house? It really scared me!

I was stunned, but finally got up the nerve to creep back towards my bathroom while this loud pounding continued with a steady beat of Bam, Bam, Bam! Just as I got to my bathroom door, I could tell without a doubt that it was coming from right under my bathroom window. Slowly, without making a sound, I sneaked up on the window to look out and when I got almost to the window it stopped! I flew to the window and opened the shade to look out but saw nothing! I went back to my bedroom, grabbed a blouse out of my closet and flew out the front door and around the house. I was running so it only took seconds to get out the door, but there was no one there when I got outside. I looked all around the neighbor's yards and no one was in sight.

My yard is totally fenced in with the gates all padlocked, so any person would have had to jump the fence. How could they have gotten far enough away that I couldn't see them? I don't think a person could have pulled that off. I don't think it was a person pounding like that on my house. I think it was a spirit or an ET, and it scared the crap out of me. For some reason, I feel more like this was a spirit rather than an ET, but I'm not sure.

We went to the party and Claudia spent the night with me as she is a teacher and needed to work the next morning, and she works close to my house. I have an alarm system with a pad by the door and in my bedroom. Every time someone opens an outside door the alarm system says "back door open" or "front door open") and it announces it through both pads.

At 6:30 a.m. the next morning the alarm woke me up saying "back door open" and I knew Claudia was leaving for work. I tried to go back to sleep because I only had a few hours of sleep. I couldn't sleep and was just lying there in bed with the door closed. About 20 minutes after Claudia left I heard some loud rustling around in my kitchen. I thought maybe she put something in her car and she was still in the house, but wondered what she was doing in the kitchen. After about 10 minutes of hearing this movement going on in the kitchen I heard an extremely loud crashing sound.

Now I was lying there wondering what Claudia broke in the kitchen. I didn't feel like getting up then, but about an hour later I got up and walked into the kitchen. There, on the floor was a decorative plaster plaque that I had hanging above the cabinet doors and it was broken in pieces all over the floor. It appeared to have just fallen off the cabinet after hanging there for years.

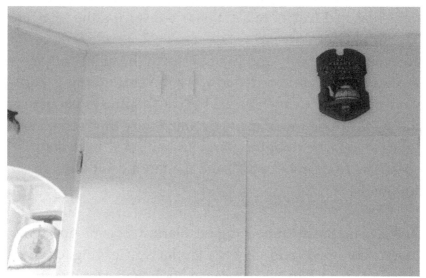
Location where plaque was on the wall

I talked with Claudia that afternoon when she got off work. I asked her if she left when she opened the door or if she come back in and did something in the kitchen. She said, "No I left right after I opened the door and I did not come back in the house." I wondered what the rustling sound was in the kitchen that lasted for about 10 minutes before the plaque fell off the cabinet and broke, and who could have done that.

October 4, 2015- Unexplained bruise
I woke up this morning and was washing my face when I noticed a bruise at the edge of my right eye on the corner. It was bright red, as if it has been freshly done, and I thought *how the heck did this happen in the night?* Then I got to looking at it and it looked like a bruise that could have been caused by an eye clamp that would be used for holding my eye open. I took a picture of it the next day and it was still there but not quite as red. It took a good amount of makeup to cover this bruise.

October 8, 2015- More bruises

This morning after my shower, I was drying off and found a large bruise in the crease area on the back of my left knee. Now how do you bruise the crease area of your knee? I have no idea this happened. I am getting so tired of waking up and finding bruises, cuts, and all kinds of marks and scars on my body. I just don't know what I can do about it, but I do feel like this is proof that *something* is happening to me. I sure wish I had started recording all these things years ago, but at least now I do have some pictures.

Jean Walker

Chapter 17

My Haunted House, Shadow People and Ghost Hunts

October 2014- Spook Night

I called this night **"Spook Night"**. Tommy was still living with me and had just started dating a girl named Edie. I went to sleep on this night only to be awaked by the house alarm going off. I knew Tom was downstairs, so I just figured he forgot the alarm was on and opened the door. I was aggravated that he woke me up, but heard him shut the alarm off. Tommy lives in the basement where he has a living room, bathroom, and bedroom and it is like his own apartment. So I just went back to sleep and in about 30 minutes the alarm went off again! I wasn't so nice this time and I opened my bedroom door and I could hear him shutting off the alarm. I yelled at him, "What the hell are you doing setting that alarm off over and over and waking me up?"

Tom said, "Mom I am telling you, I never opened that door once and I keep running up these basement steps turning the alarm off!" I have had this alarm system for five years or more and never has it ever just gone off on its own. I told him, "You've got to be kidding me, there is no way this alarm system would just go off for no reason." Tom said, "Mom I swear I don't know why it is doing it, but I haven't done anything to set it off."

We reset the alarm again and I went back to bed. This was about 11:30 p.m. and I was hoping to get some sleep, but at about 12:30 a.m. Tommy was knocking on my bedroom door. He said, "Mom I am going over to Edie's house because she is scared and she has been hearing strange

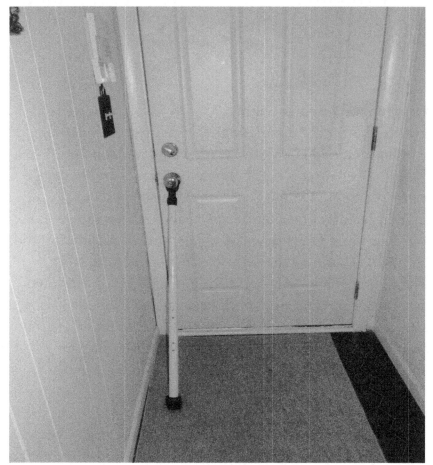

Brace under doorknob

noises in her house. I am sorry to wake you again but give me a minute to get out the door, then set the alarm again." I thought, *my God, this is the craziest night I have had in sometime, and I was so tired.* I have an alarm box right in my bedroom so I didn't even open my bedroom door. I gave him a minute to get out the back door and reset the alarm from my bedroom.

The next morning, I got up and went into the kitchen to start my coffee. I walked into the hallway to shut off the alarm and when I looked at the door it was barred from the inside. I have these heavy metal braces that go under the door handle to keep someone from kicking in the door. I just stood there in shock looking at the brace thinking how Tommy could have gotten out that door with the brace on it. It would be impossible!

I wondered if maybe he came home and didn't spend the whole night with Edie but if he did come back in, the alarm would have gone off and I would have heard it. So I looked out the door and his car was gone, then I went downstairs just to double check and he was not there. I was totally puzzled. All I could think was this is just too weird! How could this happen? I called Tommy and sure enough he was at Edie's house and he said he had never come back to the house.

Now I knew something very strange was going on, so I called the alarm company and told them my alarm was going off on its own the night before and this had never happened before. They said they would send a tech out to look at it. The alarm technician arrived that afternoon and he checked out everything in the house. He told me that there was no way could the alarm go off by itself like that. I said, "Well I am sorry but it did twice last night." The man still didn't believe me but said everything checked out fine.

Then he said, "Well I have done everything now, I just have one more test to do on it and I will be done here." The test didn't go right. It seems the alarm was going off here in my house but it was not letting the alarm company know that it was going off, so if someone had broken into my house, the alarm company would have never known to call the police!

He asked me where the phone line came into the house, so I took him out back to the phone box. When he came back in the house he retested the alarm and this time it worked correctly, calling the alarm company. He said a wire had been disconnected in the box and he hooked it back up.

The phone box has a place where you can put a padlock on it to keep anyone from getting into it. So when he left I put on a padlock. No, it would not keep anyone out of it if they really wanted to get into it, but at least I would know if someone was messing with it.

There are a couple of ways this could have happened. The most reasonable one is that I had the phone company out here working to correct some problems and they were back there in the box. So quite possibly, one of them accidentally knocked the alarm wire off or took it off and just forgot to put it back on. The other possibility would be maybe someone intentionally took the wire off, like someone interested in my MUFON cases and my files. Guess I will never know the truth for sure.

However, the big question is who is looking out for me? Someone or something had set that alarm off twice to get my attention because they knew it wasn't working right. Someone or something placed that heavy metal door brace under my door after Tommy left the house in the middle of the night. Looks like someone is really watching over me and protecting me!

More Strangeness
I have had many strange occurrences take place in my home in the 49 years I have lived here. These are just a few things

that have happened lately.

December 2014

I was in the basement running the vacuum sweeper and I turned around quickly with the sweeper in hand to clean a different area. I noticed a shadow on the ceiling, and it was huge and scary! It was all black, with a head and had its arms up by the head with its hands up and spread out.

I dropped the sweeper and yelled out, "Ohhhh" and it disappeared! It was only there for a second, but I was sure about what I saw. I was just running the sweeper and not really thinking about anything but cleaning when this happened. What a shock! I kind of caught my breath and thought about what I had seen. I decided it was gone now as I looked all around but I wasn't going to let it run me out of my own house. I just continued to do my cleaning, but was very leery of my surroundings.

After cleaning, I started to bring up my Christmas decorations which are stored in the basement. I was going up and down the stairs with boxes of decorations. About an hour after I had my scare with the shadow person looming over me, I made a return trip to the basement. As I stepped off the last step into the basement I saw what looked like a black streak go across the wall in front of me. It was dark, was about five or six feet high but very narrow, maybe only six inches wide. I call it a streak because it did not have a shape like the previous shadow had.

I just stood there, not believing what was happening. I said out loud, "Okay I have had enough of this crap for one day. I don't know who or what you are but get the hell out of my house now!" I haven't seen anything like that since, but when I am in the kitchen, which is where the basement steps are, I can sometimes feel it watching me. It won't show itself, but I can sense when it is around and watching me.

A few days before Christmas, Doug was visiting and we were sitting at the dining room table. To his right is the living room with a closet door next to the front door. We were just sitting there talking when he just jumped and looked strangely at me. I said, "What's wrong?" He said, "I just saw something black go past that closet door out of the corner of my eye." I laughed and then I told him what I had seen a week before in the basement. He seemed a little uncomfortable about what had happened, but said he was sure of what he saw. I felt like this really helped to support what I had seen a few weeks earlier in the basement was real.

Doug, whom I have known for twenty years, told me he felt that I had really been having a lot of bad luck lately and maybe these dark shadows were causing some of my problems. It did make me stop and think about all things that had been happening to me lately - could he right about the shadows?

I saw shadows in this house many years ago, and then they just stopped appearing. Now they are back, what does that mean? I really became worried about it, so I called my friend Hector Lugo who is owner and operator of the 10th Dimension Paranormal Group. I asked Hector what he thought about these black shadows appearing in my house and if they could be causing me any problems in my life. Hector didn't think these shadows would be able to harm me in any way. He said a lot of times these shadow people were just getting energy from a person and that this happens when they scare you. I am sure that one big shadow got lots of my energy when it frightened me so badly! These shadow people are thought to feed off the fear of the people they scare.

I started reading books on shadow people in order to find out more about the shadow people. There is no consensus on what these shadows really are. The reasons range from: things that can harm you, to the devil wanting to take your soul, to almost nothing at all, but most investigators say that they do seem to feed off of your fear of them. I still don't know what to make of them, but I don't like dark things looming around my house!

February 2015- Site Investigation

I decided to have Hector and his paranormal team out to my house to do an investigation to see if they could tell what was happening around here. In February 2015, Hector and his team came to my house. It was very interesting and they spent a long time just setting up equipment. I asked my son, Tommy, to come over for this because he has lived most of his 44 years in this house, too. Tommy brought his girlfriend

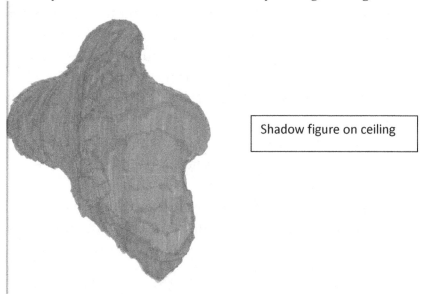

Shadow figure on ceiling

Edie over with him, so there were the three of us and

Hector's team.

One of Hector's team members, Diane, is a psychic who really helped out with our investigation. They set a large screen monitor in my dining room that all the cameras were hooked up to. The cameras were night vision cameras, so we turned out all the lights and the cameras continued to pick up everything in the house.

Hector took Tommy and two his team members to the basement where Tommy used to live. Edie and I sat in the dining room with the man running the monitor. This man said to me, "Man, you have a lot of orbs shooting around this house." I could see these orbs in the monitor and they were flying through every room of the house, even right over our heads! I was most surprised by the number of orbs that were in my bedroom as that was where the largest number of orbs could be seen.

Edie and I could hear everyone talking in the basement and we decided to join them. Diane asked me, "Who died in this house with chest pain?" Well, my husband Chet died of lung cancer about 22 years ago, and he experienced severe chest pain. She told me he was here and she could feel his terrible pain.

Then she asked, "Who was the older man that was related to you that was here." My grandfather passed away here due to his heart (more chest pain). He had been sick and came here so I could take care of him. I hired a nurse and rented a hospital bed for him. The nurse was with him when he passed away, and she said he went very easily, that he just let out a sigh and passed away. I was very close to my grandparents. My grandma passed about 6 months earlier before grandpa died. Diane said, "Your grandfather is here protecting you all the time." I really think she is right because that just sounded like something he would do. She said that sometimes grandma was here with him. I miss them both so badly and I hope she's right about them being here with me.

She told me that my second husband Chet was here, too, and he also watched over me. Chet was a big man at 6'4" and a body builder; he was an ex-Marine and a police detective. He was a very strong man until cancer took him. He was also very protective of me.

My husband Bill, who passed with cancer less than two years ago, was here too. Bill did not get along with my son and they had a real distaste for each other. This also put me at odds with Bill often because no matter what, Tommy is my only child and the love of my life.

Tommy, Edie, and I sat on the couch while the team was walking around us and questioning us. The wall straight across from where we were sitting has a bookcase with a shelf that extends out. The investigators put two flashlights and several tape recorders on the shelf.

Using the flashlights, the team would ask question that were "yes or no" questions or Tommy or myself would ask questions. Tommy asked Bill if he was still mad at him. We had a tape recorder sitting on the coffee table in front of us. We played the recording (the EVP) back after Tom asked the question. There was a voice that sounded just like Bill on the recorder and it answered Tommy by saying "No." This really seemed to give Tommy some peace in his heart to hear that answer, so I was very grateful for that answer.

Diane continued asking questions by asking the flashlights to be turned on and off for a reply. It became obvious that Bill was here, too. Hector said that most the time when we cross over all is forgiven. Diane told me she thinks Bill is here trying to make amends to me and Tommy. I guess that was Bill rubbing my back and turning on the coffee pot for me!

Diane told me that I had a lot of love around me and they were really protecting me. So now I know what that "Spook Night" was really all about. I have no doubt that my loved ones are with me all the time and that is a great comfort to me. It is amazing to me how much they can do for us even though they are on the other side. Maybe it's true that love never dies. Love is a very strong energy and can transcend even through death.

"Now I know what a ghost is. Unfinished business, that's what."

Salman Rushdie

Chapter 18

A Possible Portal

Unexplained foggy apparition in photo taken of the house

For Christmas 2015, I set up some yard decorations in November. I decided to take a few pictures of the decorations with my digital camera. Without a flash, I took a series of about seven pictures. A few days later I downloaded the pictures onto my computer. All the pictures came out crystal clear except for one very strange picture with some type of foggy apparition in it. After looking at it, I decided to send it to Margie Kay to see what she thought about it. She called me and said, "Jean I think you have a portal at your house. I remote viewed this, and when you think about all the strange things that happen at your house, this would explain a lot." She also told me I should continue to take pictures of the house.

In June 2016, and I was almost finished with this book. I wanted a picture of my house to go into this book. I chose a bright, sunny day to take pictures of the house and yard.

I downloaded the pictures and then I started looking at them. I could see something in several of my windows that I thought at first were reflections. I started zooming in on all the windows and was I surprised to see some sort of creatures in these windows. The scary thing about this is that not only were there some type of strange creatures inside my house, but they were looking out the windows at me taking the pictures! The first person I showed these to was Claudia when she came over one day. I have a 23" monitor and you can see things very clearly on it. She said, "Oh Jean, I think there really are things in this house looking out at you, but what are they? I had no idea what they were, so I sent them to Margie and she wrote back saying, "Do you remember that portal we saw in your yard? Well, I think these creatures are coming and going through your house all the time and that explains a lot about your house."

I must agree with Margie because these are very strange looking creatures. A couple of them look like aliens to me and one is very dark and could be more than one creature. Another one has two faces to it. So what the heck are they? I finally showed them to my doubting friend Doug who got rather upset and said he was afraid they were demons. Even Doug could see them.

Following are the pictures I took of the house:
Look at the living room window (first set of windows on the porch). In the first window on the left there is something white that looks like a reflection at first glance.

Front of the house

Below: Close-up of living room window showing some type of creature looking out from the inside. Note that it is behind the window, not in front of it.

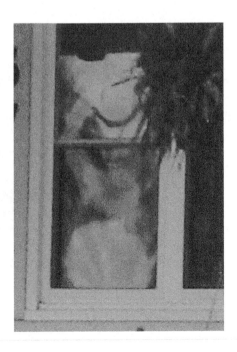

Side of house

Some of us see two heads in the photo on the previous page. The first one is very large head (reminds me of ET.

Right: Close-up of what I think really looks like an alien with large eyes and skinny neck!

Right: Left kitchen window again, there is something very dark in it maybe several things in it as it is difficult to tell. However, there is something there!

Above: A man's face at the lower left bottom of the window

More oddities at my house

One morning in February 2016, I woke up feeling very tired. When I went to make my bed I noticed there were three drops of blood on my pillow case. I went into the bathroom mirror and looked at my face and then I checked out my arms, but there was no sign of any type of injury or bleeding.

In the last week of March I discovered that my belly button had numerous little scabs on it. It felt like sand, only it was attached to my skin in my bellybutton. I looked in the mirror and it looked like little holes that were healing, kind of like needle- sized holes. It looked as if someone had been sticking me in the belly button many times with a needle. This was yet another body mystery. Who or what would be sticking needles in my belly button enough so that small scabs would appear?

In March 2016, I was lying in bed watching TV about 8:00 pm, when I heard a series of three knocks on the back side of my house, then a series of another three knocks. It sounded as if it was right next to my bed, only outside. I was a bit alarmed that this was happening again. The knocks were loud enough to be heard over the TV and almost as loud as the knocks I heard last April on the side of the house. The difference this time was they were coming in sets of three. I got my nerve up and looked out through the blinds, but I could not see anything or anyone outside. I walked through the house and looked out a lot of different windows, but saw nothing. Even though it was dark outside, my yard is well lit and I could see quite well. I have also experienced hearing knocks at the door and the doorbell ringing at the side of the house twice this month. Again, upon investigating, there was no one there.

Animals Have Souls, too

Towards the end of March 2016, I was sitting on the bench at the end of my bed putting on my shoes. My new dog, Casper, was lying in front of me. Suddenly Casper started making a low growl sound, then he started slowly moving towards the dog bed that my Pepe always slept on. Casper went from the low growl to barking frantically at the bed. I couldn't believe this was happening as I stared at the empty dog bed. But I could tell Casper didn't think the bed was empty. I really knew at that time that my Pepe was home again and lying in the bed he loved so much.

In May 2016, I was in my office area working on the computer and Casper was in his usual place in a chair right next to me as I work. I was just typing away when I heard a crash in my bedroom which sounded like something glass hitting the floor. Casper sat up and looked in that direction and then at me. I thought okay, *let's go see what that crash was about.* On my TV stand on the bottom shelf, I have a nice clear glass powder bowl that has an elephant on the lid. The lid had been knocked off somehow but was lying about a foot away from the bowl! Stranger yet, it was not broken, but how did it get knocked so far away? I knew it couldn't have been Casper because he was with me when this happened and I heard the glass hit the floor right next to Pepe's bed. I had a very strong bond with Pepe, it was almost like he was a part of me and I know he felt the same way about me.

Editor's Note: As I was editing this portion I heard a loud noise in the front part of my office, when I went to investigate I heard footsteps walking on the floor above me. I called my daughter and son-in-law and they came right over, but found nothing. As my daughter and I were standing in the front office talking about paranormal activity, a big piece of cardboard came flying of my husband's desk. We both thought this was strange timing.

This is just a gut feeling about what happened with the powder bowl, but I know animals have souls and they do return to us sometimes. I think maybe Pepe was back and knocked the lid off the bowl as he was going to his bed or maybe to let me know he was here with me. I am sure he misses me as much as I miss him. Casper has helped me a lot with my grieving, but I still miss my Pepe.

Casper looking at Pepe's bed

Glass lid off the powder bowl

When I was growing up, we had a family pet Boxer dog name Duke. He grew up with my brother and me and was just like another sibling. Duke went everywhere with us, even on camping trips and long vacations. He slept with me a lot and we loved him dearly. He passed away at the age of 13 and it was very difficult for the whole family.

At the time Duke died, I was living in the basement apartment of our home. So often after Duke died, I would be the only one home because everyone else was at work. I would hear Duke's tags rattling and him walking around the house just like he always did.

Several times I heard him running through the house upstairs with his tags rattling and I would run as fast I could out the basement door around to the front of the upstairs level, open the door and then look all around for Duke. I never found him there although I would often feel his presence.

I have experienced animals returning many times. There are still times when I feel my Siamese cat, Sheba, who lived to be 21 years old, walking on my bed when I am in it. I know she has visited many times. That was the strangest cat I ever owned. She didn't like anyone but me, and she loved her mama! She would tolerate some people, but she really didn't like anyone else and it was obvious. She always slept with me, and I know how she felt on the bed and I know when she visits me now.

May 2016

I was talking with a friend on the phone when I heard someone knocking at my door. Casper heard it too, and started barking. I told my friend to hold on while and I went to the door. It didn't take me long to get to the door and there was no one there. I hope this didn't mean the ETs would come for me tonight!

June 2016

I was jolted awake by a big crash at 3:30 a.m. Casper jumped up and ran to the edge of the bed making low growling and barking sounds and looking at me. I sleep with a .38 pistol next to me, so I jumped up and grabbed my gun. I knew for sure that something had happened because the crash was very loud. I opened my bedroom door with gun in hand and looked around for a few seconds but saw and heard nothing. At this point, I stepped out into the hallway, and looked in the bathroom. All of this area was well lit. I then looked in my office but saw nothing, so I headed into the rest of the house except for the basement. I decided to go back to my office because that was where I thought the crash originated.

I went back into my office and this time I turned the light on. Then I saw what it was- a picture had fallen off the wall and was lying on the floor with the glass broken. It was a picture of me and my brother. Doesn't it seem strange that the picture just fell off the wall and broke at 3:30 am? It is thought by some that demons will show themselves at 3:00 or 3:30 am and that paranormal and UFO activity is highest at this hour. Was this another coincidence?

Later that month I was in the basement getting some supplies and Casper was with me. I went to the utility room and was getting items off a shelf when Casper started to growl. I turned around and he was looking in the direction of the washer and dryer. Then he backed up and started barking with a louder growl. I could tell by watching Casper that he was really seeing something in that direction and he was scared. I kept looking where he was looking, but could see nothing. This is the same spot where I was standing when I saw that large, looming black shadow figure over me.

June 2016 was a busy month for paranormal experiences. I was in my office area working again on the computer and Casper was in his chair next to me. I started hearing some rustling around in my kitchen, which is at the other end of the house. I thought that it sounded like someone in my kitchen, but no one else was in the house, just Casper and me. I saw Casper lift his head up and look that direction as if he heard something as well. I finished what I was doing on the computer and then went into the kitchen about 10 minutes after hearing the rustling sound.

The sound I heard reminded me of the noises I was hearing in the kitchen the morning the plaque just mysteriously fell off the cabinet wall and broke.

I immediately noticed that the cabinet door over my stove was standing wide open! I had not been in that cabinet all day and that cabinet door is tight fitting so there is no way it could have just popped open!

What is going on in the house? It seems something is trying very hard to get my attention. What is it, an ET, a spirit, or something demonic? I think a paranormal investigation is needed again.

July 2016- The Garden and Corn Mystery

I found the center of my corn had a circle where the corn was laying down flat. I have an empty field not far from me and it's not that big, maybe five or six acres, and there are some deer in it. Last year I had to let Pepe out at 3:00 a.m. and went with him. I saw 3 deer right up against my fence and I am sure they were looking for food. The first thing I thought about was the deer must have jumped my fence and bedded down in my corn.

I only have 6 rows of corn and this circle was right in the middle of the corn. I went into the area and lifted the stalks back up and was surprised that most of them stayed up. So, thinking this was deer doing this, I didn't take a picture of it. Then about three days before I felt the vibrations, I saw where the corn was mashed down again. This time the area ran from the edge of the corn where the tomatoes were to a much larger area, kind of a rectangular shape in the corn. All the stalks were bent over lying flat on the ground. Boy, was I cussing those deer for smashing my corn!

My friend Doug came over and I ask him to come out and look at the corn where the deer were smashing it down. Doug walked all around the corn and he started pulling the corn stalks back up looking at the ground. He said, "If deer have been here, there should be hoof prints on the ground." Doug also checked out the rest of the yard but could not find any footprints at all, animal or human. He even checked out the fence saying they often leave hair in the fence because the edges of the fence are sharp, but we found no hair.

When we came back in the house, Doug said, "There is something bothering me about all this. You know I have hunted deer all my life and there are always foot prints around, but I didn't find any. Also, most deer will eat the garden stuff, but nothing has been eaten and I find that strange."

Two weeks later more strange things happened in my garden. I went out to do some work. I grabbed a stake to pull it up out of the ground so I could move it to another place. When I grabbed the stake, I could feel it vibrating so I held it for just a few seconds. Then I looked at it -thinking *what the heck was that?* I grabbed the stake again it vibrated again, only this time it didn't last for long, then it stopped. I tried to push the stake further down in the ground thinking maybe I'd feel the vibration deeper in the ground, but nothing happened.

The garden

This picture was taken after Doug lifted most of the corn stalks, so it doesn't show the pattern that was there before.

I then walked over to my zucchini plants and went to pick a zucchini. When I grabbed the end of the zucchini to twist it off the vine, it too was vibrating! As soon as I got the zucchini off the vine I felt no more vibration.

I have lived in this house for 50 years and I know for a fact there is nothing under the ground where my garden is. There are no water or sewer lines under the garden and the electrical lines come from the poles that run along the front of the property. So what the heck could be causing a vibration in the ground in my garden? Sometimes I feel like these things that are happening will make people will think I am crazy!

I got to thinking about this: I had a vibration in my garden, and corn that was laid down in a circular pattern. This reminded me of crop circles and the strange phenomena that is often associated with them. Margie contacted Nancy Talbott with B.L.T. Research. Nancy is a well-known crop circle researcher. Margie asked Nancy if she'd ever heard of anything like this with objects vibrating after a crop circle had been found. Nancy said that she was unaware of anything like that, or that crops could be picked up after they were laid down and stay up, much less continue to grow.

So now, I have a new investigation going on right at my own house. I am going to make trips out to garden at night and see if I can find anything in the corn. Doug is going to put up a camcorder on the tree next to the garden. I have more questions than answers, but I will be checking it all out and recording the results. Hopefully, we can come up with some answers and I will let my readers know the results in my next book.

"People don't believe me when I tell them I'm a magician who makes portals to other worlds. So I tell them I'm a writer instead."

Genesis Quihuis

Chapter 19

My Star Child

My son is adopted and I have had him since birth. It is almost unbelievable that someone could adopt a child that is so much like themselves. He even looks like me, and everyone is always telling me they can tell he is my son. As I explain to everyone by saying, "He is my son for sure, he couldn't be any more mine than if I gave birth to him a thousand times." Truer words have never been spoken!

Tommy is very special, not to just me, which he is, but to the world. He is the most musically inclined person I have ever known. He is a vocalist for a band, has great writing abilities and writes most of their songs, he is very handsome, has an outgoing personality, and most people find him very charming.

He is a real performer on stage, his lungs are powerful and he can hit very high notes. He is very creative in all that he does and a master in the recording studio. I have gone with him and his band when they are doing recordings. I was amazed with his talent and had no idea what a master he was in the recording studio. Tommy can single out and hear all kinds of musical things going on that I couldn't hear at all. He has a true ear for music; it is just innate in him. He has rhythm in his soul and it shows in his music. Talented people just march to their own drummer and they operate at much higher degree with their gifts than the average person.

When Tommy was in his playpen and not even a year old yet, I realized how much he loved music. He would hold on to the side of his playpen and shake his butt to the music. My mother said to me one day while watching him, "He just has music in his soul." Oh, how true that turned out to be! I bought him everything that played music when he was a kid. He had record players for tots and many other musical toys. Anything musical was always among his favorite things to play with.

Tommy and his guitar player have returned from Nashville where he has been recording his album. He has a big producer who is helping record this album and I don't want to mention his name, but it is a name everyone would recognize. I think Tommy is going to have great success in his music career and very soon. His new album is called "Rock Revolution", and the band is Jett Blakk.

I am very proud of him as he is working in Nashville with all these professional musicians and he can hold his own with his singing and writing skills. Nashville appears to be very impressed with him.

Tommy has many talents and he has, for sure, always marched to his own drummer and often paid the price for it. He is a bluesy rock singer that likes to do things his own way. He grew up listening to rock bands like the Rolling Stones and Aero Smith. Tommy can sing like Steven Tyler, maybe better than Tyler can sing it, but that is my opinion. He grew up singing in local rock bands in Kansas City, one of the best known bands he was in was called "WolfGang." He grew up during a time period of sex, drugs, and rock & roll, and I think he did them all!

One thing different about Tommy is that he has a special ability to sense danger. He calls this ability his Sixth Sense. At the oddest of times, he will stop everything he is doing and will react to what he is feeling. He tells me this Sixth Sense has saved his life many times. He now feels this gift was given to him because he is a "Star Child".

Tommy has physic abilities as well. He seems to know how to react and listen to the things going on around him. When my dad was killed in his airplane accident, I was devastated. About two days after dad had been killed, I was backing out of the driveway and I had been crying over my dad. Tommy was about 10 years old and he said, "Mama please don't cry because I saw Papa Ted last night and he said for me to tell you he is okay. He said for you to stop crying and grieving over him because he is okay."

I stopped the car and said, "What do you mean you saw Papa Ted last night?" He told me that when he had gone to bed the night before- Papa Ted came to him. He told Tommy he was okay and to tell his mama so she would stop grieving so badly. I asked Tommy if he really did see Papa Ted and he told me, "Only his head, I didn't see his body, only his head. Papa said he was in a good place and for us to stop crying over him. He said he was okay."

I was just stunned at Tommy's story and I believed him. I know my son well and he was not lying to me, he truly saw his Papa Ted that night. This was some great comfort for me to know my dad was doing okay on the other side and so soon after his death.

Tommy also had some visions when he was young and would tell me about them. I think he was really seeing things that adults are unable to see, much like my brother and I did as children. I remember at one time he even had an invisible friend who he played with which lasted for a couple of years when he was young. Who knows, maybe he was really seeing someone the rest of us could not see.

My friend Margie has met Tommy and has seen him perform. She remote-viewed Tommy and said he is going to be very successful in the music business and that he is very talented. She tells me it will all happen very soon and that when it does, he will rise to stardom very quickly. Then one day Margie said to me, "You know Tommy is a "Star Child." I didn't know what that exactly meant and I had to think about it for a few days.

I later had a realization about Tommy and I knew in my heart Margie was right. Next time I saw Margie I told her I thought she was correct and that Tommy was a "Star child". I told her that I thought the aliens knew that taking my babies had messed me up so badly that I couldn't have a child. I think they finally realized what they had done to me, mentally and physically, so they gave me Tommy. Tommy and I were meant to be together!

Margie said that my job was to raise Tommy and that because he was a Star Child he needed a special mother who could understand his psychic abilities and his musical talent. He needed someone who would encourage him, rather than discourage his pursuits.

I thought about what Margie said and it all fit together like the pieces of a puzzle, it fit and I knew it was correct. My son and I are very close and have always been. Nothing in my life has ever been as important to me as being Tommy's mom. He is my life and why God put me here on earth, to be his mother. Tommy was a very difficult child to raise and a lot of parents would have given up on raising him, but it was all worth it to me. He is my Star Child!

Tommy is my gift in life and my reason for being. I do believe he was sent here for a reason and that Tommy and I needed each other to get through life. Tommy is a Star Child sent here with his great musical talent to enlighten the world with his music and his heart. I feel Margie Kay was right on with her remote viewing of Tommy and me. So, if the aliens did send him to me, it was also through the grace of God. After figuring all this out with Margie's help, I was drawn to a book titled, Star Children by Nikki Pattilo. I think there was a real reason I was so drawn to this book. This book explains how there are three kinds of star children, the Indigio, Rainbow, and Crystal children. The very first type she talks about in her book is the Indigo children, and this describes Tommy through and through.

Nikki explains how these souls will bring peace, topple corruption, and how they will shift dimensional consciousness in the coming years. Even Tommy's birth year of 1970 was correct for Indigo children and almost everything in that chapter, from being extremely talented to many other gifts, fit with Tom.

She explains how these people are here on a group mission to assist in this rebirth into a higher dimension for Earth. I would strongly recommend this book for parents that suspect they could have a "Star Child". There are many of them out there and they do have special gifts and talents to contribute to the world. So at least some of my puzzle is starting to fit together, but I still have many pieces floating around out there.

Tommy Lee Barton performing with Jett Blakk at KC Fox 4 Morning news show

Tommy Lee Barton and Jett Blakk with news anchor Mark Alford

Afterword

I don't know if the mystery of UFOs will be resolved in my lifetime, but I sure hope something big will happen that cannot be denied. I feel our government keeps us in the dark for many reasons, some of them are secrets that probably do need to be kept quiet from the public for defense reasons.

But there are still so many questions out there that need to be answered, like what are UFOs? Where do they come from? What is their agenda with or for humans?   Are they here with good intentions? Are they harmful to humans? What is it about all the secrecy with the government that they will not share it with us? How long have aliens been involved with the human race? Why do some humans know they are here, but not others? There is no end to list of questions that need to be answered. Along with all the other UFO investigators, I am trying to do my small part in finding out some of the answers. Writing this book is another way of exposing them and looking for the truth.

Through my efforts of trying to educate myself and do investigations of UFOs my conclusion for now is that they are as different as we are. There are good cops, bad cops, good teachers, bad teachers, many different races of humans on this Earth and so it is the same with aliens. There are many different types or species of aliens. Like every species. some are good, some are bad.

The Nordic type of aliens is the kind of alien I remember showing me my son. They are thought to be from the Pleiades (Plee-a-deez) which is a cluster of stars found in the constellation body of the bull, Taurus. They are tall, blonde, blue eyed aliens and wear white robes. The Nordic aliens are thought to be the kinder of the aliens and are often found to be healers.

There are the "Greys", which some people think are the workers. They do jobs for other type of aliens that includes the larger "Greys", but they are not always so kind to humans. They often are the ones that hurt humans in examinations or they take the humans to the larger Greys to do the examinations. These are the aliens with the large heads and very large almond shaped eyes. The smaller, more fragile "Greys" with the spindly bodies, are the ones that usually take us from our beds. They are the more robotic type of "Greys" who show little to no emotion. They also help in conducting all types of experiments on humans. They are the workers for the larger Greys. The larger Greys do show more emotions (than the smaller Greys) and will often converse with their abduction victims.

The Greys have been known to do some kind things for humans like healing, but they could have their own reasons for doing this. They often conduct horrifying experiments and procedures on us. What their reasoning for this, I do not know, but I suspect it is the same reason humans conduct horrible experiments on the lower animals on our planet. Being a member of the human race, I am not so proud of that and I find it to be inhumane. Not to mention, how we humans hurt and kill each other.

These Greys seem to have one agenda that is clear in that they want to create a *human/alien hybrid species*. So, one must ask, what is it about humans that aliens want to incorrupt into their race? Perhaps it is our stronger human bodies or because humans have emotions or for something we possess in our DNA that they do not have. We can only guess at their agenda for now.

I do not think of the Greys as being good for us because of what they do to humans, but we really don't know what they are all about yet. However, I do know they have great control over humans. They are capable of wiping our minds clear so we can't remember what they did to us and to paralyze us so we can't move.

They don't think of the consequence by doing this to the humans, it is all about what the Greys want for us and do to us. I can't help but wonder what the hybrid species think of humans, since they are half human. Will the hybrids want to experiment with humans in the same ways as the Greys have? Perhaps the hybrids will want to make peace with the human race and help us in our endeavors. On the other hand, maybe they will want to breed with us humans until our species is not human anymore, and humans would be developed into some other species all together.

Then there's the Reptilian type of aliens who have different shapes and are often described as having scales. They are very ugly by our standards and are often considered to be very mean. It is reported that they are sometimes disguised as police and medical personal and they do great harm to humans. So they do have the power to take on a human form but I have heard their eyes are sometimes different, in that their pupils run vertical instead of being round. They are also referred to as the "Reptoids". For some reason, this type of alien scares me the most and I just get chills thinking about them. Maybe because the reptiles here on Earth are cold-blooded, and this Reptilian race of aliens seem to be so cold-blooded towards humans.

However, I have heard of a few of the Reptilians being helpful to humans, but the opposite is more likely to happen. I just feel I would never want to have anything to do with them no matter what the situation as I just wouldn't trust them. I have heard that the Reptilian aliens are often found to be working in the police departments and in the hospitals. This would allow them to have a great amount of control over a lot of humans and do more harm to humans. It is believed that this species of aliens like to live underground such as in tunnels, caves, storm drains, and other underground facilities.

There are also reports about the "Insect" type of aliens. They resemble praying mantis' and other ant-like creatures here on Earth. This is another very scary type of alien to me. Most humans don't care much for insects. Most of the reports I have heard about with this type of alien are not good ones, but that they are found to be a mean and torturous type of beings. Can you even imagine seeing or being at the mercy of a huge praying mantis? This is like the things nightmares are made of, large insects! They are often reported to have large, black eyes and sometimes they have more than just two eyes. They are just creepy!

On a happier note, I heard a story on TV the other night, it went something like this: To the small kitten, a veterinarian must seem like a terrible tortures creature for what they are doing to the helpless kitten, but the reality of what the vet is doing is what is best for the kitten. This immediately made me think of our relationship with the aliens. We just don't really understand what they are up to in our lives.

There are many other alien races than what I have mentioned here. The types I have talked about are the more commonly known ones that we hear about the most in our field of investigations. There are many good books out there that explain much more than what I have highlighted here for you on alien races.

I think maybe my resentment towards what the aliens did to me physically is why I hunt them now. They took my babies and exploited me and now I want to exploit them. I think we are getting close to proving they do exist and some of what their agenda is.

MUFON is a good example of this with so many investigators working hard to get some answers. They (aliens & government) put obstacles in our way often to stop us in our investigations. I have heard of everything from bugging phones and computers, to having great tragic events happening in our personal lives, even putting some whistle blowers in mental institutions or causing them to get cancer. All these things are huge distractions for investigators and, of course, often stops us in our tracks for exposing what we know or what we are trying to find out.

Now that I have retired from teaching, I have a lot more time to work on MUFON investigations and to delve into my own personal happenings. I now have the time to write books, read, investigate, educate myself and try to put some of the puzzle pieces in my life together. Even though they may put obstacles in my life, I am going to keep investigating and working to expose them for as long as I can.

So as my favorite saying goes, "Eyes to the Sky!"

"If it is just us, seems like an awful waste of space."

Carl Sagan

Right: Ted & Jean as children

Left: Ted & Jean
August 2005

WORKS CITED LIST

Jean Walker's first-hand experiences are the foundation of her research.

Clelland, Mike. *The Messengers: owls, synchronicity and the UFO abductee.* Richard Dolan Press, USA, 2016

Hollis, Heidi. *THE HAT MAN. The True Encounters of Evil Forces*, USA, 2014

Kloetzke, Chase and Dolan, Richard. *Admissible: The Field Manual for Investigating UFOs, Paranormal Activities and Strange Creatures*, USA, 2014

Kay, Margie. *Gateway to the Dead: A Ghost Hunter's Field Guide, Second Edition.* Nocturna Press. USA, 2013

MUFON Field Investigator's Manual, Mutual UFO Network, Inc., USA, 2011

Oldham, Bret. *CHILDREN OF THE GREYS.*

Offutt, Jason. *Darkness Walks: The Shadow People Among Us.* Anomalist Books, USA, San Antonia* New York, 2009

Pattillo, Nikki. *CHILDREN OF THE STARS.* Ozark Mountain Publishing, USA, 1966

Websites:

www.spooklight.freewebspace.com/custom4.html.

http://www.astraltravelsecrets.com/astral/esperiences.aspx

http://en.wikipedia.org/wiki/Astral-projection

http://www.mythsandlegends.wikia.com/wiki/fairy

http:// www.mythsandlegends.wikia.com/wiki/Elves

About the Author

Jean Marie (Myers) Walker was born in Kansas City, Missouri where she still resides. Jean is a MUFON Star-Team Field Investigator, speaker, author, and educator. She is also Section Director and Secretary for the MUFON, Kansas City Chapter and has investigated many cases in Missouri. Jean's great grandmother was a well-known psychic in the Kansas City area, and Jean has followed through with many of her grandmother's traits.

Jean is an educator who taught middle school Science for the Kansas City, Missouri School District. She has a BA from Central Missouri State University in Elementary Education, Middle School Certification, Science, and Language Arts. She has a Master's in Education and Computers from Webster University in Kansas City, Missouri.

After teaching Science for almost 20 years Jean is now retired. In retirement, she finally has the time to follow up on a lifetime of strange experiences. Jean became a MUFON Field Investigator in 2011. She is working diligently trying to help find out what is going on in our universe and here on Earth. In this book, Jean has been able to put into writing many of her lifetime experiences with UFOs and alien abductions since childhood along with her brother's experiences. She is also speaking out about many of the psychic and paranormal events taking place in her family.

Jean has been doing speaking engagements concerning her UFO investigations. She feels the need now to help to educate the public concerning what is really happening with the UFO phenomena. She is hoping to educate and help counsel others about the phenomena and the fact we are not alone!

Jean started writing a cookbook titled "Out of This World Recipes." She also has plans to write more books and continues to educate herself in the study of UFOs. She hopes by working with MUFON and other field investigators, and by doing research in this field, she will increase her knowledge base in these areas of study.

UN-X MEDIA

Publications by Un-X Media:

Haunted Independence by Margie Kay 2013 – 2016
Family Secrets by Jean Walker 2017
The Kansas City UFO Flap by Margie Kay 2017
Mysterious Missouri by Margie Kay (coming soon)
Un-X News Magazine 2011-2016 in print
Un-X News Magazine 2016 digital online at
www.unxnews.com
More publications coming soon

Visit www.unxmedia.com for more information

Un-X Media is currently taking book submissions.
We publish non-fiction books about unexplained
phenomena. Please check the website for writer guidelines.

Contact:
editor@unxmedia.com
816-833-1602
www.unxnmedia.com

Made in the USA
Coppell, TX
25 June 2020